The
TEX-MEX
COOKBOOK

THE
TEX-MEX
COOKBOOK

by
Elizabeth Blakeley

drawings by Ruth Ann Keil
cover design by
Elizabeth Blakeley

Library Of Congress Cataloging in Publication (CIP) data.

ISBN 0-9644411-1-X
Published by:

Caxton House Publishing Company
P.O. Box 15345
San Antonio, Texas 78212

First publication, 2000.
Second printing, 2001.
Third printing, 2003.

To order additional copies of this book complete the form on page 159 and return with $11.95 plus $3.00 for shipping and handling to:

Caxton House Publishing Co.
P.O. Box 15345
San Antonio, Texas 78212

or fax to: 1 (866) 371-6212

TO REGGIE
AND
JANICE

Table of Contents

INTRODUCTION

In San Antonio we are extremely proud of our Tex-Mex cooking. The combination of seasoning, texture and color used in Tex-Mex cooking is unique to San Antonio and South Texas. No where else in the world will you find this particular style, taking from the influences of border Mexican cooking, interior Mexican foods and Mexican American dishes.

From salsa to sangria, fajitas to flan, and margaritas to mole, these are the traditional recipes of San Antonio style Tex-Mex. This regional cuisine has roots in many sources and is widely varied, creating a sophisticated blend of tastes that is sure to please the most distinguished palate.

San Antonio prides itself in being a city of many cultures. The Mexican-American culture is shared and enjoyed by all who live here. Nowhere is this more prevalent than in the Tex-Mex cuisine enjoyed throughout the city by people of all backgrounds.

Tex-Mex cooking is sure to please you and your guests as it has those who live here in San Antonio. The recipes are suitable for a family meal as well as any occasion with guests. Watch out! Like many here, you may find it habit forming.

The Tex-Mex Cookbook

CHILES: SOME LIKE 'EM HOT

The term peppers is a misnomer which came from the early Spanish explorers looking for black pepper in the East. They named the chiles they found in the Indies peppers because of the spicy taste. The correct term for the type of "peppers" used in Tex-Mex cooking is chiles. I have, however, used the term "peppers" when referring to such chiles as jalapeños and serranos because in San Antonio they are more commonly referred to as peppers. For the purposes of this book, peppers and chiles refer to the same type of ingredient, except when black pepper is called for.

ANCHO:

The ancho chile has a wonderful, moderately hot, smoky flavor. It is a dried poblano chile, about 4 1/2 inches long and 2-3 inches wide. To use them you must remove the seeds, stems and veins and rehydrate them by poaching them in water. The poaching takes about 1 hour. After poaching, the skin should be removed gently with your fingers (wear rubber gloves to protect your fingers). The pulp that remains is what is left to cook with. The pulp is usually ground in a food processor or blender to make a paste.

CARIBE:

The caribe looks similar to the jalapeño, but it is bright yellow in color. It is milder than a jalapeño, but hotter that a bell pepper. You can use it as a substitute for a jalapeño in any recipe if you like a milder taste.

CASCABEL:

This chile comes dried and has a dark, brownish red color. It is hotter then other dried chiles and can be used in enchilada sauces and chili when a hot flavor is desired. The cascabel is grown in a

variety of shapes from long and flat to small and rattle-shaped. Before using, you must rehydrate them by poaching in a small amount of water for about an hour. Then remove the seeds and veins and peel the skin off. Wear rubber gloves while peeling the chiles to protect your hands from skin irritations. The pulp is ground in the food processor or blender to make a paste. This paste is what you use in the recipes.

CHILE DE ARBOL: "Chiles of the tree":
A very small bright red chile that is very hot. Adds a spicy taste to menudo.

FINGER HOT PEPPER:
Long and slender resembling a finger, this chile is mostly green with some orange at the tip. Mildly hot. Can be used to make pepper sauce.

GOLD BELL PEPPER:
The sweetest and mildest of the bell peppers. Adds brilliant color and a distinctive sweet flavor to many dishes. May be served fresh with a dip or in salads, as well as grilled, roasted, sautéed or baked.

GREEN BELL PEPPER:
This chile is sweet, with a slightly spicy flavor. Used with onion in many Tex-Mex dishes and sauces. A perfect pepper for stuffing.

GREEN CHILES:
Canned green chiles are roasted and peeled poblano peppers. Some of the recipes give instructions on roasting and peeling the poblanos. If this process is too time consuming or difficult, you should use the canned green chiles.

HABANERO:

Also called the scotch bonnet pepper. The hottest of the hot chiles, the habanero is 100 times hotter than the jalapeño. Sold dry or fresh. Used primarily in sauces and chili. Use rubber gloves when handling to avoid skin irritation.

JALAPEÑOS:

Jalapeño chile peppers are used extensively in Tex-Mex cooking. They are used fresh or canned. Most of the recipes use fresh jalapeños. If, however, the recipe calls for canned jalapeños, do not use fresh because the canned ones are pickled and taste different than the fresh. Canned jalapeños are indispensable on nachos.

NEW MEXICO OR ANAHEIM:

This long and slender chile is shiny and green like the poblano when fresh, but can be found dried and dark in color. It measures 6-7 inches in length. The New Mexico chile varies in heat, but is generally mild to moderate. It is perfect for stuffing and for flavor in uncooked salsas. Also, known as the Rio Grande pepper and the California pepper.

PASILLA:

The pasilla, which gets its name because it looks like a raisin, is similar to the poblano. It comes dried and is mild to hot. The pasilla is used in enchilada sauces, tamales and mole. Before using the dried pasilla, they must be rehydrated, peeled and then ground in the food processor or blender.

PEQUIN:

These tiny red chiles are extremely hot and come dried in the store. They are used primarily in hot sauces.

POBLANO:

The poblano is a dark green chile, triangular in shape, that measures 5-6 inches long and approximately 2 inches wide. They are used extensively in Tex-Mex cooking because of the sweet, smoky flavor. Poblanos are great to use in chile rellenos. They

are found fresh in the produce section of the grocery store or canned and already peeled as green chiles. Before using them, you should remove the tough skin. This is done by roasting the chiles in the oven at 400° for about 20 minutes to cause the skin to blister. After roasting, the chiles must be steamed by removing them to a bowl and covering with plastic wrap or by wrapping them with a damp cloth. Let the chiles steam for about 20 minutes. The poblanos should then be ready to peel. The skins should come off easily if you hold them under running water. As with any chile, you should wear rubber gloves to peel them to avoid skin irritations.

RED BELL PEPPER:
This is the mature form of the green bell pepper. It is most commonly available in the fall. When roasted, this pepper has a wonderful smoky flavor. The color and taste make the red bell a great choice in salads and salsas.

SERRANO PEPPERS:
The serrano chile is similar to the jalapeño, except that it is smaller and hotter. They are green, red or orange in color, but usually come green in the grocery store. The serrano is used in salsas such as Pico de Gallo and picante. Since these chiles are extremely hot you should remove the seeds and veins before using. They should be chopped very fine. Use rubber gloves when handling serranos and other fresh chiles to avoid skin irritation.

HANDLING CHILES:

FRESH GREEN CHILES: Large, fresh green chiles such as poblano and New Mexico must be seeded and skinned before using. This is done by a process of first roasting the chiles. You can roast the chiles in the oven at 400° or on the grill for about 20 minutes or until the skin blisters. The chiles should be turned during this time so that they can blister evenly. Once roasted, the chiles should be promptly removed to a bowl and covered with plastic wrap or wrapped in a damp towel to allow the chiles to steam. The steaming process takes 10 to 20 minutes. I usually allow 20 minutes. Now the skin can be removed from the chiles. Remove the seeds by slitting the chiles open and running them under tap water. If you are using the chiles for stuffed chiles and chile rellenos, leave the stems on, otherwise remove the stem.

Canned green chiles already have their skins, stems and seeds removed, and work well in any recipe calling for roasted, skinned green chiles such as the poblano. I prefer the fresh chiles, however, if you have the time and determination to go through the preparation process.

Small green chiles such as jalapeños and serranos do not need to be skinned before using. You should, however, remove the seeds, stems and inside ribs because they contain most of the heat. You should always use rubber gloves when handling these chiles to avoid skin irritation. The canned chiles such as jalapeño peppers are quite different than the fresh because they are pickled. You should only used the canned chiles when called for specifically.

DRIED CHILES: Many chiles are available today in the dried form. They are wonderful to use and are preferred over the powdered chile if you have the time to prepare them. Dried chiles must have their seeds and stems removed, and be rehydrated before using them. The dried chiles sometimes have dust on them from the packaging process. You should always wash them first. Then cut them open and remove the seeds, ribs and stems.

To rehydrate the chiles they should be poached in enough water to cover for about 20 minutes. Cool them and peel off the skins with your fingers. The remaining pulp is what is used in the recipes. The pulp is usually ground in a food processor or blender until it is a thick smooth paste. If you have trouble removing the skins after poaching, you should grind the chiles in the food processor or blender and then strain the pulp to remove the skins. Good luck with this process it is difficult at first but should get easier with experience. If you do not want to handle dried whole chiles, use ground chile.

GROUND CHILE: Ground chile is available in either hot or mild and you can use either according to your taste. Ground chile should not be confused with chili powder. The latter has other ingredients such as cumin and oregano added.

MAIL-ORDER SOURCES FOR MEXICAN CHILES AND SPICES:

San Antonio TEX-MEX Co.
PO Box 15345
San Antonio, Texas 78212
(210) 325-3601
fax 1 (866) 371-6212

email: elizabeth@satexmex.com

www.satexmex.com

CHEESES: MEXICAN QUESO

The recipes in this book use cheese extensively. When available, you should use the following Mexican style cheeses to get the authentic Tex-Mex flavor. The Mexican style cheeses have sophisticated flavors from light to creamy to aged.

ASADERO: Similar to mozzarella, this cheese can be used in quesadillas, or melted and poured over vegetables.

COTIJA: My personal favorite, cotija is an authentic, dry, aged, full-flavored cheese. Similar to Greek feta cheese, it is great to crumble over salads or over beans. It is also great in enchiladas, flaquitos or in pasta.

ENCHILADO: This cheese is strong and hard. It is encased in powdered chile. Enchilado can be used in enchiladas, nachos or as a cheese sauce.

FRESCO: This is a white cheese that adds an authentic Mexican flavor to any recipe. You can crumble it over huevos rancheros, or use it in chile rellenos or enchiladas verdes.

MANCHEGO: Manchego has a rich, mellow flavor and is great in quesadillas and other Tex-Mex dishes.

PANELA: This is an authentic Tex-Mex cheese. Great for tacos, salads and quesadillas. Low in fat, sodium and cholesterol.

QUESADILLA: This cheese has a unique flavor and is excellent for melting. It is great in quesadillas, enchiladas, chile rellenos, and nachos. Queso quesadilla can be melted in the microwave and makes an excellent cheese sauce for vegetables and pasta.

APPETIZERS

CEVICHE

Ceviche is a light and refreshing seafood appetizer that won't leave you too full for the main course.

2 1/2 pounds of a mixture of any of the following seafood:
     fish filets, shrimp, crab meat, scallops
2 cups fresh lime juice
4 tomatoes peeled and chopped
1 (4 ounce) can diced green chiles
1 large purple onion finely chopped
2 tablespoons olive oil
2 tablespoons red wine vinegar
1 jalapeño pepper, seeded and finely chopped
1 clove garlic, minced or pressed
1/4 cup pitted, sliced black olives
1/2 cup chopped fresh cilantro
1 teaspoon oregano
1 teaspoon ground cumin
1 teaspoon freshly ground black pepper

Cut seafood into bite sized pieces. Marinate in lime juice 4 to 5 hours in refrigerator. Drain lime juice. Mix with remaining ingredients and refrigerate overnight.

Drain excess juices and serve on lettuce leaves or in a dessert cup. Accompany with crackers, toast rounds, or tortilla chips.

The seafood in this recipe is not cooked before marinating in the lime juice, but the marinating process itself actually cooks the fish. In other words, this is not Mexican sushi.

CHILE CON QUESO

Chile con queso is the classic cheese dip for tostada chips.

1 pound processed American cheese
1 (4-ounce) can chopped green chiles
1 tomato peeled and finely chopped
1 small onion finely chopped

Melt cheese in a double boiler or in the microwave. Add green chiles, tomato and onion. Stir. Serve warm with tortilla chips. May be kept warm in a chafing dish or over a food warmer.

Variations. Substitute 1 (10 ounce) can diced tomatoes and green chiles for tomato, green chiles and onion; add one clove crushed garlic; add 4 tablespoons picante sauce; or add 1 can of chili without beans.

CHILEQUILES

In Spanish chilequilas means "broken up old sombrero", which describes the broken pieces of corn tortilla used to make this dish.

1 medium onion, chopped
1 clove garlic, minced or pressed
2 tablespoons olive oil
1 (14 1/2 ounce) can diced tomatoes
salt and pepper
1 (8 ounce) can green chiles, whole
1 package corn tortillas (or 1 package of tortilla chips)
oil to fry tortillas
2 cups cheddar cheese, grated
1 pint sour cream

Sauté onion and garlic in oil until onion is clear. Add tomatoes and salt and pepper to taste. Simmer 10 minutes. Remove seeds from chiles and slice into 4 inch strips. Cut tortillas into triangles and fry in hot oil until crisp. Drain. Place half of the tortilla chips in a 9"x13" baking dish. Layer tomato mixture, chiles and cheese. Make a second layer of each, ending with the cheese. Heat in a 350° oven for 30 minutes or until bubbling and the cheese is melted. Remove from oven and top with sour cream. Place under broiler for a few minutes until lightly browned. Serve hot.

Variation. You may add 2 cups of chopped, cooked chicken to make this recipe a main dish.

Appetizers

EMPANADAS

Empanadas are turnovers that are made in a variety of ways. These empanadas are bite-sized and filled with meat, cheese and mild seasoning.

1/2 pound ground beef or cooked chicken, shredded
1/2 cup onion, chopped
1 clove garlic, minced or pressed
2 tablespoons olive oil
1 cup cheddar cheese, grated
1/4 cup picante sauce
1 teaspoon chili powder
dash of Tabasco sauce (optional)
salt to taste
4 9-inch pie crusts

Preheat oven to 450°. Sauté meat, onion and garlic in oil until onion is clear and meat is browned. Add cheese, picante sauce and seasonings. Heat thoroughly. Cut pie crusts into 2 1/2 inch circles with a biscuit cutter. Spoon 1 teaspoon of meat mixture in the center of each circle. Fold in half and seal by pinching the edges with your fingers. Bake 10-12 minutes until golden brown.

Makes 4 dozen appetizers

FLAQUITOS

Flaquitos are tightly rolled, cigar shaped, tacos. They can be served as an appetizer or as a main course dish.

1 small onion, chopped
1/2 pound lean ground beef
1 teaspoon salt
1 teaspoon ground cumin
1 clove garlic, minced or pressed
1 tablespoon picante sauce
oil for frying
18 corn tortillas
2 cups grated cheddar or Monterey Jack cheese

Sauté onion and ground beef in a heavy skillet until beef is browned and onions are clear. Add salt, cumin, garlic and picante sauce. Simmer for 10 minutes.

Heat 1 inch of oil in skillet and dip corn tortillas into oil briefly (1 second), using tongs. Drain on paper towels.

Place 1 tablespoon meat mixture and 2 tablespoons of grated cheese on one end of each tortilla. Roll tightly in a cigar shape, and place into a greased baking pan, seam side down. Bake at 400° for 20 minutes.

Serve with picante sauce, guacamole, or sour cream.

Makes 18 small servings

FLAUTAS DE POLLO

Flauta means flute in English, and describes the shape of this tightly rolled chicken taco.

1/2 cup onion, chopped
2 cloves garlic, minced or pressed
3 tablespoons butter
1 cup cooked chicken, shredded
2 tablespoons picante sauce or salsa
1 to 2 tablespoons chicken stock
1 poblano chile, cut into 12 strips
12 corn tortillas
1 cup sour cream (optional)
1 cup picante sauce (optional)
1 cup guacamole (optional)

In a large skillet sauté onion and garlic in butter. Add shredded chicken and picante sauce. Keep mixture moist with needed amount of chicken stock. Heat thoroughly.

Heat 1/2 inch oil in skillet. Using tongs, dip each tortilla in the hot oil for one or two seconds to soften. Drain on paper towels.

Place one tablespoon of chicken mixture and one poblano chile strip on each tortilla and roll tightly (like a cigar). Place side by side, seam side down, on a shallow baking dish. Bake at 400° for 20 minutes, until crisp.

Serve with salsa, guacamole or sour cream.

Makes one dozen

GREEN CHILE SQUARES

This recipe makes a quiche-type snack with a Mexican twist.

2 (4 ounce) cans green chiles
4 cups sharp cheddar cheese, grated
6 eggs, beaten
2 tablespoons prepared mustard
2 teaspoons Worcestershire sauce
dash of Mexican hot sauce
1/2 teaspoon paprika

Remove seeds from chiles and lay flat on the bottom of a greased 9 x 13 inch pan. Mix cheese, eggs and mustard, Worcestershire, and hot sauce. Add salt and pepper if desired. Pour over peppers and sprinkle with paprika. Bake at 350° for 25 minutes. Cut into bite sized squares.

GUACAMOLE

Guacamole is a Tex-Mex classic. This blend of avocado and lime juice is primarily used as a dip with chips, but it's also great as a salad dressing, condiment, or garnish. The traditional recipe is very simple.

2 large Haas avocados (Haas avocados are best, they are dark and bumpy)
1 teaspoon fresh lime juice
salt to taste

After the avocados are ripened, cut them in half and remove the seed. Remove the skin and discard. Mash the meat with a fork or masher until fairly smooth (it is OK if there are some lumps). Add the lime juice and salt and mix well. Serve immediately. The seed may be placed in the middle of the guacamole, large side down and half way in, to help reduce discoloration.

Variations. Add any of the following: one teaspoon finely chopped onions , one half chopped tomato, one crushed garlic clove, one teaspoon picante sauce, one teaspoon mayonnaise or sour cream.

NACHOS

The nacho is the Tex-Mex ambassador of goodwill to the rest of the world. Many a Tex-Mex habit began with nachos. They can be made in a variety of ways with any of your favorite toppings. Get creative.

Basic Recipe:
1 package round tortilla chips
1 (15 ounce) can refried beans
1/2 pound shredded cheddar cheese
1 (10 ounce) can sliced jalapeño peppers

Spread refried beans on each tortilla chip. Sprinkle chips with shredded cheese. Place one jalapeño slice on each chip. Heat in 400° oven until cheese is melted.

Variations. Substitute Monterey Jack cheese for cheddar cheese. Add any of the following ingredients: shredded chicken, chili, taco meat, shrimp, crab meat, purple onion, or black olives.

Tortilla chips can be made at home by deep frying corn tortillas that have been cut in quarters, the shape of triangles.

PANCHO VILLA'S BIRTHDAY CAKE

This is a layered dip that is served with tortilla chips. When assembled, the dip should look like a white birthday cake.

Make two layers of each of the following ingredients on a round serving dish.

2 large cans of jalapeño bean dip
1 pound ground beef, browned, with one package taco seasoning added
5 large avocados mashed with a teaspoon of lime juice
3 large tomatoes, chopped
1 small can of ripe black olives, sliced
2 cups grated cheddar or Monterey jack cheese
8 ounces sour cream

Finish the dip with the sour cream spread on top to resemble icing on a cake.

Serve with plenty of tortilla chips.

PICADILLO

Picadillo is a meat dip that resembles taco filling in appearance, but has its own unique flavor that sets it apart from the ordinary.

1/2 pound ground beef
1/2 pound ground pork
1 small onion, chopped
1 cup water
1 teaspoon salt
1/2 teaspoon cinnamon
1 teaspoon sugar
1/2 teaspoon paprika
1/2 teaspoon oregano
1/2 teaspoon cumin
2 cloves garlic, minced or pressed
1 small can tomato paste
1 large (14 1/2 ounce) can diced tomatoes
3 small potatoes, peeled and diced
1 small jar diced pimentos
1/2 cup raisins
3 jalapeño peppers, seeded and minced
1/2 cup slivered almonds, toasted

Brown meat with onion until onions are clear. Drain. Add water, seasonings, garlic and tomato paste. Mix well and simmer, covered, for 30 minutes. Add remaining ingredients, except almonds. Stir and simmer for another 30 minutes. Add almonds and simmer for another 10 minutes. Drain excess liquid. Serve hot in chafing dish with tortilla chips.

QUESADILLAS

This Tex-Mex treat begins with flour tortillas that are filled with cheese, onion and jalapeños, then browned in oil or butter. Other fillings may be added, making this a versatile appetizer or main dish.

16 flour tortillas
1/2 pound cheddar, Monterey Jack or Mexican white cheese, grated
1 onion, sliced in rings
1 jalapeño pepper, seeded and chopped
Oil, butter or cooking spray for browning

Heat a large skillet or griddle to medium high heat. Lightly oil the pan with oil, butter or spray. Lay a tortilla flat on the skillet. Sprinkle 1 tablespoon cheese, 1 slice of onion and several pieces of jalapeño on top. Cover with another tortilla. Cook until cheese has melted, turning once. Remove from heat and cut up into triangles. Serve immediately.

Serves approximately 25 as an appetizer

Variations: Experiment with quesadillas and find a filling that is your favorite. Some of the fillings that are most popular are: cooked chicken, taco meat filling, refried beans, sautéed onion, black olives, fresh chopped cilantro, picante sauce, chopped tomato, chopped green chilies, fresh crab meat and cooked shrimp. The possibilities are endless.

You may also use this as a main dish recipe serving 6-8 slices to each person.

RATITOS

These stuffed jalapeños derive their name from the fact that they resemble a small rat if you have a vivid imagination or have been sampling the margaritas too long.

1 (7 ounce) can whole jalapeños
1 pound chopped cooked shrimp or crab
1 cup buttermilk
1/2 cup flour
1/2 cup cornmeal
1 teaspoon chili powder

Cut jalapeños down one side and remove the seeds. Leave stem on. Stuff with shrimp or crab. Mix flour, cornmeal and chili powder. Dip each stuffed jalapeño in buttermilk, then dredge in flour mixture. Fry in hot oil until golden brown.

TEXAS SUNSET DIP

In color, this dip resembles the glow of a Texas sunset. You can serve it any time of the day.

3 large packages of cream cheese
3 (2 ounce) jars pimentos, drained and chopped
1 (10 ounce) can of diced tomatoes and green chiles, drained
1 (8 ounce) jar picante sauce, drained
1-2 tablespoons hot sauce
3 cloves garlic, minced or pressed
salt and pepper to taste

Combine all ingredients and blend thoroughly. Start with 1 tablespoon of hot sauce, then add more if desired. Serve with tortilla chips.

SALADS

BLACK BEAN SALAD

3 (15 ounce) cans of black beans
1/2 cup olive oil
Juice of one lime
3 tablespoons red wine vinegar
4 cloves garlic, minced or pressed
1/2 cup purple onion, chopped
1/4 cup fresh cilantro, chopped fine
1 cup salsa
1/2 cup black olives, sliced or halved
2 cans whole kernal corn (optional)

Drain beans and place in a bowl. Combine oil, lime juice, vinegar, and garlic and pour over the beans. Add onion, cilantro, salsa and olives and toss. Chill several hours.

Serves 10-12

You may serve this an an appetizer with tortilla chips.

CACTUS SALAD

Nopalitos are the edible pads of the Opuntia cactus. If found fresh, select the thinnest and smallest pads.

2 cups cactus (nopalitos), fresh or canned, drained and
   washed
3 tomatoes, chopped
1/4 cup purple onion, chopped
1/4 cup fresh cilantro, chopped
1 jalapeño, seeded and chopped

1/4 cup olive oil
1/2 cup red wine vinegar
1 clove garlic, minced or pressed
1 teaspoon dried tarragon
freshly ground black pepper to taste
1 small jar pimento, finely chopped
1 head of romaine or salad bowl lettuce.

If using fresh cactus, remove thorns, chop, and cook in salted water until tender. Drain the cactus and wash until skin is removed.

Mix first 5 ingredients. Set aside. Combine remaining ingredients, except lettuce, and blend well to make dressing. Pour dressing over cactus mixture. Chill and marinate in the refrigerator until ready to serve.

Line salad plates with lettuce leaves. Top with marinated salad. Garnish with slices of lemon and lime.

Serves 6-8

CUCUMBER SALAD

On those hot summer days, this cool salad does the trick.

3 tablespoons olive oil
3 tablespoons red wine vinegar
Juice of 1/2 lime
1 teaspoon oregano
1/2 teaspoon cumin
1 teaspoon Worcestershire sauce
2 cloves garlic, minced or pressed

3 cucumbers, peeled, seeded and chopped
3 tomatoes, chopped
1/2 cup black olives, sliced or halved
1 small purple onion, chopped
1/4 cup fresh cilantro, chopped
1/2 cup feta or Cotija cheese, crumbled.

Combine first 7 ingredients to make a dressing.

In a salad bowl, mix the remaining ingredients. Pour dressing all over and toss. Chill well for one hour or more before serving.

Serves 8 to 10

FIESTA SALAD

This salad makes the perfect side dish for any Tex-Mex meal. It's colorful and perfect for an outdoor buffet.

Juice of 1/2 lime
3 tablespoons olive oil
3 tablespoons red wine vinegar
3 cloves garlic, minced or pressed
1 teaspoon dried oregano
1 teaspoon Worcestershire sauce

2 tomatoes, chopped
1 small purple onion, chopped
2 cans whole kernel corn
1/4 cup fresh cilantro, chopped
1 green bell pepper, chopped
1 red bell pepper, chopped
1 zucchini, diced
1 or 2 serrano peppers, seeded and minced (optional)

Combine the first 6 ingredients to make a dressing. Mix the dressing with the remaining ingredients blending well. Chill and serve.

Serves 8 to 10

MANGO SALAD

Mangos are a tropical fruit with a light, sweet taste and a creamy texture. This sweet, congealed salad makes a terrific accompaniment to any Tex-Mex meal.

3 packages lemon jello
1 cup boiling water
1 large jar or can mangos with juice, all to measure 3 cups
juice of one lemon or lime
8 ounces of cream cheese, softened and cut in chunks

Dissolve jello in 1 cup of boiling water.

Purée mangos and juice, and lemon or lime juice in food processor or blender. Add jello and cream cheese chunks. Blend thoroughly.

Place in a greased 9x13 inch Pyrex dish and chill in refrigerator at least one hour.

Serve by cutting into squares and placing on top of lettuce leaves. This salad may also be prepared in a ring type gelatin mold.

Serves 10-12

PASTA SAN ANTONIO

OK, so they weren't eating pasta at the Alamo. If they'd had it they would have served it like this.

1 pound dried pasta, corkscrew or fuselli
1 teaspoon olive oil
1/2 cup red onion, chopped
1 cup celery, chopped (optional)
1 red bell pepper, chopped
1/2 cup black olives, sliced or halved

1 cup salsa
3 tablespoon olive oil
3 tablespoons fresh lime juice
1 teaspoon dry mustard
1/4 cup fresh cilantro, chopped fine
1/2 teaspoon oregano
2 cloves garlic, minced or pressed
1 teaspoon Worcestershire sauce

Cook pasta according to package directions. Drain and run under cold tap water to cool. Drain again. Toss with olive oil to prevent sticking. Add onion, celery, bell pepper and olives. Toss.

Combine remaining ingredients, blending well to make a dressing. Pour over pasta mixture and chill before serving.

Serves 8 to 10

TACO SALAD

This one's really a meal. It's the Tex-Mex version of a chef's salad.

1 pound ground beef
1 teaspoon salt
1 1/2 tablespoons flour
1 1/2 tablespoons chili powder
1 1/2 cups water
1/2 teaspoon ground cumin
2 cloves garlic, minced or pressed

1 head of lettuce, iceberg or romaine
1 small onion, chopped
1 cup cheddar cheese, grated
1 medium tomato, chopped
1 cup bottled or homemade ranch dressing
2 cups tortilla chips crumbled
1 avocado, coarsely chopped
1/2 cup black olives, sliced or halved
1 teaspoon minced jalapeño peppers (optional)

Brown ground beef in a medium sized skillet. Drain. Add salt, flour, chili powder, water, cumin and garlic. Simmer over low heat until thickened, stirring occasionally.

Shred lettuce into small pieces and place in a large salad bowl. Add beef, onion, cheese, and tomato, mixing well. Add dressing and toss until well coated. Chill.

Just before serving, add remaining ingredients, as desired. Toss gently. Serve immediately.

You may substitute cooked chicken in this salad for the ground beef.

Serves 4 to 6

SALAD DRESSINGS

Try one of these unique blends to give a new twist to your tossed salads.

CILANTRO DRESSING

2 ounces olive oil
2 ounces red wine vinegar
4 cloves garlic, minced or pressed
1/4 cup chopped cilantro
1 teaspoon Worcestershire sauce
1/2 teaspoon oregano
1 teaspoon sugar
1 teaspoon fresh lime juice

Mix all ingredients well and chill before serving. Serve poured over your choice of salad greens.

FIESTA DRESSING

This dressing is great as a dip for fresh, raw vegetables as well as over salad greens.

3 tablespoons mayonnaise
3 tablespoons sour cream
2 tablespoons red wine vinegar
2 cloves garlic, minced or pressed
1 teaspoon Worcestershire sauce
1/4 cup salsa or picante sauce
1/2 teaspoon cumin
1/2 teaspoon paprika
1/2 teaspoon oregano
juice of 1/2 lime

Blend all ingredients together well and chill before serving. Serve on a bed of salad greens, tomato, and onion.

POPPY SEED DRESSING

The light, sweet taste of poppy seed dressing over mixed greens make a great contrast to the spicy Tex-Mex main dishes. Once you try it you will use it over and over again. You also use this dressing over mixed fruits and melons. One favorite way to make a side salad is to pour it over chunks of cantaloupe and avocado.

1 cup oil
1/3 cup vinegar
3/4 cup honey
1 teaspoon salt
1 teaspoon dry mustard
1 green onion
1 tablespoon poppy seeds

SOUPS

AVOCADO SOUP

This is a chilled soup with a creamy texture. It adds a light touch to a spicy Tex-Mex menu.

3 large ripe Haas avocados
2 cans chicken broth
2 cups half and half
1/2 teaspoon salt
1/2 teaspoon onion salt
1 teaspoon ground red chile powder
1/4 teaspoon ground nutmeg
fresh ground black pepper to taste
juice of two limes

Peel and seed avocados and puree to a pulp in a food processor or blender. Add one can of chicken stock. Puree again until smooth.

Transfer to a large bowl. Add remaining chicken stock, half and half, seasonings and lime juice. Beat all with a wire whisk.

Cover and refrigerate several hours until chilled through. Serve cold.

Serves 6-8

BLACK BEAN SOUP

The pinto bean is still the staple in traditional Tex-Mex cooking, but its Caribbean cousin, the black bean, is gaining ground quickly through recipes like this one.

1 pound dried black beans
1 quart chicken broth
8 ounces of bacon diced or 2 ham hocks
1 medium onion, chopped
1 small carrot, chopped
2 stalks celery, chopped
2 serrano peppers seeded and minced
1 clove garlic, minced or pressed
salt and pepper to taste
2 teaspoons chili powder
1 teaspoon ground cumin
1 tablespoon chopped cilantro
2 tablespoons Worcestershire sauce
lemon slices (for garnish)

Toppings
sherry to taste
sour cream
minced chives

Rinse beans and cover with chicken broth. Add bacon or ham hocks, onion, carrot, celery, serrano peppers and garlic, and simmer 2-6 hours or until beans are tender. Remove bones and puree in blender or food processor, one cup at a time, until smooth. Return pureed mixture to pot and add remaining ingredients except toppings and garnish. Ladle into individual bowls and add desired toppings just before serving. Garnish with lemon slices.

Serves 4-6

SOPA CALABACITA

The calabacita is a wonderful, versatile green squash that resembles zucchini, but is rounder and has a more distinct flavor. You may substitute zucchini squash in this recipe if you are unable to find fresh calabacita locally.

3 pounds lean pork, cubed
1 medium onion, chopped
2 cloves garlic, minced or pressed
1 tablespoon olive oil
1 teaspoon whole comino seeds, crushed
1 (16 ounce) can whole tomatoes
1 (10 ounce) can Rotel tomatoes, diced
3/4 cup water
1 green bell pepper, cut into 1/4 inch strips
3 pounds calabacita (Mexican squash)
1 (16 ounce) can whole kernel corn
salt and pepper to taste

Toppings
picante sauce
crumbled corn tortillas or tortilla chips
grated cheddar or Monterey Jack cheese
chopped onion

Brown pork in oil with onion and garlic. Add comino, tomatoes, Rotel tomatoes, water and bell pepper. Add salt and pepper to taste. Simmer 10 minutes. Wash and dice calabacita. Add to the meat mixture. Simmer 10 minutes. Add corn and simmer 5 minutes. Add toppings just before serving. Serve with hot tortillas.

Variation. You may use chicken breast meat in place of pork in this recipe.

SOPA ELOTE

This creamy corn soup seasoned with green chiles will warm your spirits on cold winter days.

1 onion, chopped
2 cloves garlic, minced or pressed
1 tablespoon butter
2 cans whole kernel corn
3 cans chicken stock
1 red sweet bell pepper, chopped
1 small can chopped green chiles
salt and pepper to taste
1 cup cream

Toppings

    corn kernels
    chopped green onion tops
    crumbled bacon

Sauté onion and garlic in butter until clear.

Puree corn and 1 cup of stock in blender or food processor until smooth.

Combine above with remaining stock, sweet pepper, and green chiles in large pot and simmer 10 minutes.

Fold in cream until blended and warm, but do not boil.

Garnish with corn kernels, chopped green onion tops or crumbled bacon.

SOPA FRIJOLE

Sopa frijole or bean soup is a standard Tex-Mex beginning to a traditional dinner and also makes a satisfying lunch on its own.

1/2 pound bacon
1 onion, chopped
2 cloves garlic, minced or pressed
1 jalapeño, seeded and minced
2 cans (14 1/2 oz.) tomatoes, diced
1 pound pinto beans, soaked, cooked and drained
2 cans (10 3/4 oz.) chicken broth
1 teaspoon ground cumin
Salt and pepper to taste

Toppings
2 cups grated cheddar or Monterey Jack cheese
sour cream
crumbled bacon

Fry bacon in a large pot, remove and crumble, reserving drippings. Sauté onion, garlic and jalapeño in reserved bacon drippings. Add diced tomatoes.

In a blender or food processor, puree the cooked beans. Add beans and chicken stock to tomato mixture. Season with cumin, salt and pepper. Simmer 15 to 20 minutes.

To serve, ladle soup into bowls. Top with cheese, crumbled bacon and sour cream.

Serves 6-8

Variation: You may substitute 1 can diced Rotel tomatoes if you like a spicier dish.

GAZPACHO
(A COLD TOMATO SOUP)

In the hot summer months there is hardly a more re-freshing appetizer or lunch dish than a bowl of chilled gazpacho. You will be surprised at how fulfilling a chilled soup can be when you try this recipe.

1 1/2 cup tomato juice or V-8
1/2 cup beef stock
1 tablespoon red wine vinegar
3 tablespoons olive oil
1 clove garlic, minced or pressed
1/2 teaspoon salt
2 ribs of celery sectioned
1 medium onion, quartered
5 ripe tomatoes, quartered or (1, 14 1/2 ounce, can diced tomatoes)
1 large cucumber, peeled and chopped
1 sweet bell pepper, seeded and quartered
1 tablespoon cilantro, minced
fresh ground black pepper to taste
1/2 teaspoon ground cumin

Toppings
croutons
sour cream
finely chopped chives
chopped hard-boiled eggs
minced shrimp
cold minced chicken
cold minced ham
sliced avocado

Combine all ingredients, except toppings, in blender or food processor. Blend until smooth, yet lumpy. Chill thoroughly. Serve chilled. Garnish with choice of toppings.

CREAM OF JALAPEÑO SOUP

This is a wonderful variation of the classic creamy cheese soup. Don't be afraid of the jalapeños. After cooking they are mild enough for novices.

4 tablespoons butter
1 large onion, chopped
1 large carrot, peeled and finely chopped
1 large green bell pepper, seeded and finely chopped
3 fresh jalapeño peppers, seeded and finely minced
3 tablespoons flour
3 cups chicken broth
2 cups cream
1 cup Monterey Jack cheese, grated
1 cup cheddar cheese, grated

In a large saucepan, melt 2 tablespoons butter and cook onion, carrot, green bell pepper and jalapeños on low heat until tender.

In a pot, melt remaining 2 tablespoons of butter. Stir in flour and cook, stirring constantly, 2 minutes. Gradually stir in broth and cream. Increase heat and bring to a boil, stirring occasionally. Reduce heat and simmer until thickened.

Stir in both cheeses and vegetables. Heat through until cheeses are melted. Serve immediately.

You may add 1 (4 ounce) can diced green chiles for a spicier version.

Serves 4-6

Soups

MONTEREY JACK CHEESE SOUP

Monterey Jack cheese and green chiles blend to make this a creamy, heart-warming recipe.

1/2 onion, finely chopped
1 clove garlic, minced or pressed
4 tablespoons butter
4 tablespoons flour
2 cups milk
1 cup chicken stock
1 cup cream
2 cups Monterey Jack cheese, grated
1 (4 ounce) can chopped green chiles

Sauté onion and garlic in butter until onion is clear. Add flour and stir until blended. Gradually add milk and chicken stock, stirring constantly, until thickened.

Add cream and cheese, stirring constantly over low heat. When cheese is melted add green chiles. Stir and serve immediately.

Serves 4-6

SOPA POBLANO

The roasted poblano chile makes the smoky flavored seasoning in this soup. For roasting and peeling instructions, see the section on handling chiles in the introduction, page 14.

1/2 pound lean pork, cut into 1/2 inch strips
1 tablespoon oil
1/2 medium onion, chopped
1 small can whole kernel corn
1 chile poblano, roasted, seeded, peeled and sliced into thin strips
1 small zucchini squash, thinly sliced
3-4 green tomatillos, peeled and chopped
1 clove garlic, minced or pressed
1 quart chicken stock
salt and pepper to taste
1/2 teaspoon cumin
1 large Haas avocado, thinly sliced
1/2 cup grated parmesan cheese

Toppings

tortilla chips crumbled
pico de gallo
Parmesan cheese
salsa
sour cream

Sauté pork in oil over medium heat until browned. Add onion, corn, poblano, zucchini, tomatillos, garlic and chicken stock. Simmer 20 minutes or until vegetables are tender. Before serving, add salt, cumin, avocado and cheese. Garnish with toppings of your choice.

Serves 4

SOPA de PAPAS

This potato soup is good enough to make an Irishman speak Spanish.

6 slices of bacon, cut into pieces
6 medium sized potatoes, peeled and quartered
2 medium onions, chopped
1/2 cup chopped celery
1 teaspoon salt
1/2 teaspoon black pepper
10 cups water

2 tablespoons butter
1/2 cup cream or half and half
1 teaspoon fresh cilantro, minced
1 small can chopped green chiles

In a large sauce pan combine first 7 ingredients. Bring to a boil. Cover and simmer until potatoes are tender.

Strain, reserving stock. Puree vegetables and bacon in food processor or blender with 2 cups of stock. Add back to remaining stock. Beat with a wire whisk until blended. Melt butter and stir into soup with remaining ingredients.

Reheat over a low fire until warm, being careful not to boil.

Serves 8-10

TORTILLA SOUP

This soup is a local favorite and is served in many restaurants around San Antonio. You may serve it as an appetizer or a main dish.

2 large whole chicken breasts
1 can chicken broth
1 can beef broth
1 medium onion, chopped
1 green bell pepper, chopped
1 jalapeño pepper, seeded and minced
2 cloves garlic, minced or pressed
1 tablespoon olive oil
1 large can diced tomatoes
1 can Rotel tomatoes and green chiles, diced
1 can whole kernel corn (optional)
1 small can tomato paste
1 can tomato soup
1 teaspoon ground cumin
1 teaspoon chili powder
1 teaspoon oregano
1 teaspoon salt
1/2 teaspoon lemon-pepper seasoning
2 teaspoons Worcestershire sauce

Toppings

chopped green onion
1 package tortilla chips
1 cup grated sharp cheddar cheese
sour cream

Poach chicken breasts in chicken broth and beef broth for 20 minutes or until firm. Remove breasts from broth. Reserve broth. Remove meat from bones and shred or chop. Set aside.

Sauté onion, peppers and garlic in oil until tender. Add chicken breasts and remaining ingredients, including broth.

Simmer 30 minutes to 1 hour. When ready to serve, ladle soup into individual serving bowls and add tortilla chips that have been broken in two or three pieces. Top with a sprinkle of green onions, grated cheese and sour cream.

For a more authentic version that is just a little more trouble, cut corn tortillas into narrow strips and toast or fry them until crisp. Use the strips instead of tortilla chips.

MAIN DISHES

ANTICUCHOS

Anticuchos are marinated beef and pork shish kebobs that are grilled over hot coals. The meat should be allowed to marinade one to two days. These are served during the San Antonio Fiesta.

1 cup red wine vinegar
1 cup beef broth
1 teaspoon salt
1 teaspoon freshly ground black pepper
2 serrano chile peppers, seeded and minced
2 cloves garlic, minced or pressed
1/2 teaspoon oregano
1/2 teaspoon ground cumin
2- 3 pounds lean beef, cut into 2 inch cubes
2-3 pounds lean pork, cut into 2 inch cubes
oil for basting
wooden skewers

Prepare marinade by mixing the first 8 ingredients. Place meats in a shallow container or pan and pour over the marinade. Cover and place in the refrigerator for 1 to 2 days.

Place the meat on wooden skewers alternating beef and pork. Brush with oil and grill over hot coals until done (about 8-10 minutes), turning once.

Serves 10-12

ARROZ CON POLLO

This recipe is as authentically Tex-Mex as they come. When you want a home style Tex-Mex meal, Arroz Con Pollo is a great choice.

1 frying chicken, cut into serving pieces
3 tablespoons olive oil
2 cloves garlic, minced or pressed
1/4 cup onion, finely chopped
1 sweet bell pepper, chopped
1 cup rice, uncooked
1 (14 1/2 ounce) can tomatoes, diced
1/2 teaspoon salt
1/4 teaspoon black pepper
1/4 teaspoon ground cumin
2 cups chicken broth

Season chicken pieces with salt and pepper. Brown chicken in oil. Remove chicken and sauté garlic, onion, bell pepper and rice until the onions are clear. Add tomatoes, black pepper, cumin and chicken broth. Place chicken pieces back in the pot and simmer over low heat until liquid is absorbed and chicken is tender (20 minutes).

Variations

Instead of using chicken pieces, place chicken in a pot with salt and 1 teaspoon poultry seasoning and simmer until tender, 35-40 minutes. Remove bones and skin from chicken. Save the stock to use in the recipe. Add chicken to remaining ingredients and continue with the recipe.

You may also add 1 teaspoon chopped cilantro.

Substitute 1 can Rotel diced tomatoes and green chiles for canned tomatoes for a spicier flavor.

CHALUPAS

Chalupas are fried corn tortillas that are left flat, the same as a tostada. They are then topped with refried beans, meat, lettuce, tomato, cheese and guacamole.

BEEF CHALUPAS

12 corn tortillas
oil for frying
1 pound ground beef
1 teaspoon cumin
1 tablespoon chili powder
1/2 teaspoon salt
1 clove garlic, minced or pressed
2 cups refried beans
2 cups cheddar or Monterey Jack cheese, grated
3 cups iceberg or romaine lettuce, shredded
1 cup chopped tomato
1 cup onion, chopped
1 cup guacamole, see page 27 (optional)
1 cup picante sauce, see page 132, or bottled picante sauce

Heat oil in a small frying pan on high heat, and fry tortillas one at a time until crisp. Drain on paper towels.

Brown ground beef in another frying pan with cumin, chili powder, salt and garlic. Heat refried beans in a pan or in the microwave.

On each fried tortilla, spread 1 tablespoon refried beans. Top with beef, lettuce, tomato, onion and cheese as desired. Serve with fresh salsa.

Serves 6

CHICKEN CHALUPAS

Chicken chalupas can be made by substituting 3 cups of cooked chicken for beef in the above recipe. Cook the chicken in a small amount of water that has been seasoned with salt and pepper. Shred the chicken with your hands until it is stringy (or chop coarsely with a knife). Assemble the chalupas like the beef chalupas.

CHICKEN FIESTA

Tex-Mex meets Italian in this exciting pasta dish.

8 boneless, skinless chicken breast halves
1 onion, chopped
1 green bell pepper, chopped
1/4 cup olive oil
2 cups chopped tomatoes
2 cups salsa or picante sauce
1 pound linguine, cooked in boiling water 10 minutes and drained
2 cup cheddar cheese, grated
2 cups black olives, sliced
1 cup green onion, chopped

Grill or broil chicken breasts until almost done.

Sauté onion and pepper in the olive oil until onion is clear, about 5 minutes. Add the chicken, tomatoes and salsa and simmer until heated through, about 3 minutes.

Place hot, cooked pasta on a serving platter. Spoon chicken mixture over pasta and cover with cheese, olives and green onion.

Serves 6-8

CHICKEN SALPICÓN

Salpicòn is a seasoned, shredded meat dish, used primarily as a filling for soft, flour tortillas or on top of tortilla chips. The following recipe can be made with roast beef as well as chicken breasts.

10 large chicken breast halves
3 cloves garlic, minced or pressed
1 bay leaf
1 (14 1/2 ounce) can tomatoes
1/4 cup fresh cilantro, chopped
salt and pepper to taste
1 (8 ounce) bottle Italian salad dressing (or equivalent amount
    of homemade)
8-10 dried red chiles, seeds and stems removed (See
    notes on dried chiles in introduction)
1 clove garlic
2 onions, chopped
1 cup canned green chiles, diced
1 (14 ounce) can gabanzo beans, drained
1/2 pound Monterey Jack or other Mexican cheese, grated
2 avocados, cut into strips
3 tomatoes, cut into wedges
fresh cilantro sprigs for garnish (optional)

Poach chicken in enough water to cover, adding garlic, bay leaf, canned tomatoes, cilantro, salt and pepper. Simmer until tender, approximately 20 minutes.
In another pot, cover dried chiles with water and simmer 1 hour. Remove and discard skins. Drain and place in a blender with onions, one garlic clove and 1 cup chicken broth reserved from poaching chicken. Blend until smooth. Strain and combine with remaining chicken broth. Simmer 45 minutes. Remove chicken from the bone and shred. Place chicken in a 9"x13" baking dish. Add salad dressing to the chile mixture and pour over the chicken. Cover and marinate overnight.
When ready to serve, drain liquid from chicken and place in a serving dish. Layer with chopped chiles, gabanzo beans, cheese, avocado and tomatoes. Garnish with fresh cilantro sprigs. Serve cold with plenty of tortilla chips or warmed flour tortillas.

CHILES RELLENOS

Chiles Rellenos are stuffed chiles that are battered and fried. Their unique taste and texture make them well worth the time to prepare.

8 large poblano peppers (you may substitute canned green chiles)
1/2 pound Monterey Jack cheese or white Mexican queso asadero
1 cup flour
1 teaspoon baking powder
1/2 teaspoon salt
1/2 cup corn meal
2 eggs, beaten
Oil or shortening, enough for 2 inches deep in your frying pan.

Roast peppers in 400° oven for 20 minutes or until skin blisters. Remove to a bowl and cover with plastic wrap to cool. When cooled, peel off skin with fingers. Slit open the sides carefully and remove the seeds. Leave the stems on.

Cut the cheese into 8 long narrow strips. Place one strip into each chile. Heat oil in pan. Meanwhile, mix flour, baking powder, salt and corn meal. Dip each chile into the beaten egg, and then into the corn meal and flour mixture. Fry in oil, turning once, until golden. Drain on paper towels. Serve immediately with tomato salsa or salsa verde.

Serves 4

MEAT FILLED CHILES RELLENOS

1 pound beef stew meat or boneless chicken breast
4 cups water
1 teaspoon salt
2 teaspoons ground coriander
1/2 teaspoon ground cloves
2 cloves garlic, minced or pressed
1/2 onion, chopped
1 cup raisins
1-2 tablespoons olive oil
8-10 poblano peppers (or canned green chiles)
1 cup flour
1/2 cup corn meal
1 teaspoon baking powder
1/2 teaspoon salt
2 eggs, beaten
1 cup milk
oil or shortening for frying

Poach meat in water until tender. Drain and chop in food processor. Add seasonings, garlic, onion and raisins. Sauté in oil.

Roast fresh chiles 20 minutes at 400°, until skin blisters. Place in bowl and cover with plastic wrap. Let steam in bowl for 20 minutes. Peel chiles, leaving stems on. Roasting and peeling is not necessary if using canned chiles. Slit and remove seeds. Stuff chiles with meat mixture. Mix remaining ingredients, except oil, to make a batter. Stir well.

Heat 2 or more inches of oil in frying pan to 375°. Dip the chiles in the batter. Place into oil, gently, and fry until golden brown. Drain on paper towels and serve immediately with salsa or green tomatillo sauce.

Serves 4 to 6

Variation: You can make this recipe without frying by layering the ingredients in a greased casserole as follows: 1/2 batter mixture, poblano chiles, meat mixture and remaining batter mixture.

CHILI CON CARNE

Chili is the Tex-Mex dish known all over the world. Serve chili with hot corn bread and you've got a completely satisfying meal.

6 dried red chili pods (ancho or pasilla) or 6 tablespoons
        ground chile
1 tablespoon oil
2 pounds chili meat (coarsely ground beef)
3 cloves garlic, minced or pressed
1/2 onion, chopped
1 (14 1/2 ounce) can of tomato sauce
2 cans beef broth
1 1/2 teaspoons ground cumin
1 1/2 teaspoons oregano
1 teaspoon salt
1 1/2 teaspoons paprika
1 1/2 teaspoons ground red pepper (optional)
2 tablespoons masa flour
1 (15 oz.) can pinto beans (optional)

Toppings
        1 cup grated cheddar or Mexican white cheese
        tortilla chips
        1 onion, finely chopped

Wash chiles, remove the stems, slit open and remove the seeds. Simmer in hot water until skin loosens (about 1 hour). Cool. Peel and discard skins. Puree pulp in a blender or food processor.

Brown meat with oil, garlic, and onion. Add the tomato sauce, broth and the remaining ingredients (except the flour). Add the chile pulp or ground chile. Simmer for 1 hour.

Mix the flour with 1/4 cup water to make a smooth flowing paste. Add this mixture and beans, if desired, to the chili and simmer for 20-30 minutes. Serve in bowls topped with grated cheese, tortilla chips and/or chopped onions.

ENCHILADAS

Enchiladas are the foundation of classic Tex-Mex food. To make the enchiladas, tortillas (corn or flour) are filled with meat and/or cheese and rolled tightly, then placed side by side in a shallow casserole and covered with sauce. They come in a wide variety and vary according to the tortilla, sauce, cheese, and meat that you choose to use. The red tortillas that you see in San Antonio restaurants and food markets are corn tortillas to which ground chile is added for color. These tortillas can be used as well. You will enjoy enchiladas as a main dish for your family, as well as for entertaining guests.

ENCHILADAS CON QUESO

This is the classic Tex-Mex style enchilada. Filled with robust Mexican cheese and smothered in a red chile sauce, these enchiladas show the sophisticated taste of authentic Tex-Mex cooking.

3 dried ancho chiles or 1 tablespoon mild ground chile
1/4 cup olive oil
1 tablespoon paprika
2 cloves garlic, minced or pressed
1/2 teaspoon ground cumin
1/2 teaspoon oregano
1/2 cup flour
2 cans chicken broth
12-15 corn tortillas
1 pound cheddar or Monterey Jack cheese, grated
1 medium onion, chopped fine

Red Chile Sauce

Cut the chiles lengthwise and remove the seeds and the stem. Poach them in boiling water until the skins begin to blister and loosen, about 1 hour. Cool. Remove the chiles from the water and carefully peel off the skin with your fingers and discard. Puree the pulp of the chiles in a food processor or blender.

Heat the oil to medium hot. Sauté the paprika, garlic, cumin, and oregano in the oil for one minute. Add the flour slowly, stirring constantly, and cook until browned. Add the pureed chile pulp or ground chile and chicken broth and simmer until thickened (approximately 15 minutes). This sauce can be kept refrigerated until ready to use.

Enchiladas

Prepare the enchiladas by first dipping the tortillas, one at a time, briefly, into hot oil to soften. Do not over heat. You may also soften the tortillas by placing in a microwave safe dish, covering tightly with plastic wrap, and cooking in the microwave on re-heat setting for two minutes. This will save calories by reducing oil.

Put one teaspoon of the sauce into each tortilla. Add one table-spoon of cheese and one teaspoon of chopped onion. Roll up the filled tortillas tightly and place in a greased casserole dish with the seam side down. Top with the remaining cheese, on-ion and sauce. Bake at 350° for 30 minutes or until bubbly and cheese has melted.

Serves 6-8

CRAB AND AVOCADO ENCHILADAS

The light taste of crab and avocado make the perfect enchilada for a light luncheon or summer supper.

1/2 onion, finely chopped
2 cloves garlic, minced or pressed
1/2 sweet bell pepper, finely chopped
2 tablespoons butter
8-10 ounces fresh crab meat
2 ripe avocados, mashed
1 pint sour cream
1/2 teaspoon salt
cayenne pepper to taste
12 flour tortillas
1 cup grated Monterey Jack, Queso Fresco or other Mexican white cheese
1/2 cup sliced black olives

Sauté onion, garlic and sweet bell pepper in butter until onions are clear. Add crab meat, mashed avocados, 1 cup of the sour cream, salt and pepper. Blend well.

Heat tortillas individually on a hot griddle or skillet to soften, or in microwave, covered with plastic wrap, 2 minutes on reheat setting. Fill each tortilla with crab meat mixture and roll tightly. Place rolled tortillas seam side down in a buttered casserole dish. Cover with remaining sour cream. Sprinkle with grated cheese and black olives.

Bake at 350° for 20 minutes. Serve immediately.

Serves 6

ENCHILADAS RANCHERO

Ranchero sauce has a tomato base, seasoned with green chiles, oregano and cumin. Although light in texture, the seasonings make this an enchilada full of Tex-Mex flavor.

1 medium onion, chopped
1 clove garlic, minced or pressed
2 tablespoons olive oil or bacon drippings
1 (10 ounce) can diced tomatoes and green chiles
1/2 teaspoon salt
1/4 teaspoon oregano
1/4 teaspoon ground cumin
Oil to soften tortillas
12 corn tortillas
1 pound grated white Mexican cheese (Monterey Jack, Fresco, Asadero or Quesadilla)
2 cups cooked, chopped chicken or ground beef (optional)

Ranchero Sauce
Sauté onions and garlic in oil or bacon drippings until clear. Add tomatoes, green chiles and seasonings. Simmer 10 minutes. Adjust seasonings.

Enchiladas
Heat 1/4 inch of oil in a small skillet. Dip each tortilla in the oil to soften. You can also dip each tortilla in the warm sauce to soften. This will save calories.

Place 2 tablespoon of grated cheese at one end of each tortilla to fill (or use 1 tablespoon cheese and 1 tablespoon meat). Roll each tortilla tightly and place in a 9 x 13 inch greased casserole dish, seam side down. Pour ranchero sauce over the top and sprinkle with the remaining cheese.

Bake at 350° for 30 minutes or until bubbly and cheese has melted.

Serves 6

ENCHILADAS MOLE POBLANO

Mole comes to us from Mexico. It is said that the recipe originated with the Catholic nuns who created the sauce for festivals, by using all of the ingredients on hand. The chocolate used in this dish thickens the sauce and takes the heat out of the chiles. Mole has a distinct, unusual taste that exemplifies the complex flavors in Mexican style sauces. You may wish to use bottled mole sauce that can be found in the Mexican food section of your grocery store if you do not want to make your own.

2 whole chicken breasts
water to cover breasts
1/2 teaspoon poultry seasoning
1 teaspoon salt

4 ancho chiles
4 pasilla chiles
2 onions, quartered
2 cloves garlic, peeled
3 tablespoons blanched almonds
1/4 cup raisins
1/4 teaspoon coriander
1/4 teaspoon ground clove
1/4 teaspoon cinnamon
1 teaspoon chopped cilantro
1 tablespoon sugar
1 tortilla
1 (14 1/2 ounce) can tomatoes, peeled and diced
1/4 cup olive oil
1 can chicken broth or 2 cups reserved stock from poaching the meat
2 ounces bitter chocolate
1/2 teaspoon salt
12 corn tortillas
1/2-1/3 pound grated Mexican white cheese (Cotija,

Fresco, Quesadilla, Asadero or Enchilada)

Cook chicken breasts in enough water to cover. Season with salt and poultry seasoning. Simmer 20 minutes. Reserve 2 cups of stock. When chicken has cooled mince the chicken with a knife or shred with your fingers.

Mole
Wash chiles, remove seeds, stems and veins. Simmer in 2 cups of hot water for 1 hour. Peel off skins and discard. Pour pulp into blender and puree until smooth. Add onions, garlic, almonds, raisins, spices, cilantro, sugar, tortilla and tomatoes. Do not blend all at one time if this will over fill your blender or food processor. Do several batches.

Heat the oil in a large skillet. Cook the blended mixture in the oil 5 minutes, on medium heat, stirring constantly. Add the reserved 2 cups of broth and the chocolate. Add salt to taste. Cook until the sauce is thickened and the chocolate is melted.

Enchiladas
Heat the tortillas by dipping them in hot oil, one at a time. You may also heat them in the microwave, covered with plastic wrap, for 2 minutes on reheat setting.

Oil a 13x9 inch casserole dish.

Prepare the enchiladas by placing 1 teaspoon of sauce at one end of a tortilla, add one tablespoon of the chicken breast meat. Roll tightly and place side by side in the casserole dish, seam side down. Cover with remaining sauce and sprinkle with the cheese.

Bake at 350° for 30 minutes, until heated through.

Serves 6

ENCHILADAS VERDES

Green tomatillos make a light and tangy sauce that combine with chicken, cheese and sour cream to make this a light and mild enchilada dish.

1 large onion, chopped
3 cloves of garlic, minced or pressed
3 tablespoons olive oil
1 pound tomatillos (green tomatoes), husks removed and chopped
1/4 cup chopped fresh cilantro
1 jalapeño pepper, seeded and chopped fine
1 teaspoon sugar
1 teaspoon oregano
1 teaspoon basil
1 teaspoon ground cumin
1 teaspoon salt
1 1/2 cups cooked, boned and shredded chicken
12 corn tortillas
2 cups grated Monterey Jack cheese, or other white Mexican cheese
2 cups grated cheddar cheese
1 pint sour cream

Tomatillo Salsa Verde

Sauté chopped onion and garlic in olive oil. Add tomatillos and simmer until soft and thickened. Add cilantro, jalapeño, sugar and seasonings.

Enchiladas

Grease a large casserole with oil. Dip the tortillas one at a time in the sauce for a minute to soften. (The traditional method of softening the tortillas is to fry them one at a time in hot oil, turning once, about 30 seconds on each side. Be careful not to over fry them. They should not be hard. I dip them in the sauce because this reduces the fat.)

Fill each tortilla with a tablespoon of chicken and a tablespoon of cheese. Roll up the filled tortillas and place in the casserole seam side down. Cover with the remaining sauce and then with the remaining cheese. Bake at 350° for 30 minutes or until bubbly. Top with sour cream.

Serves 4-6

TEX-MEX ENCHILADAS

Cheese, onion and chili make the perfect combination for this down home, Tex-Mex enchilada dish.

6 dried red chili pods (ancho or pasilla) or 6 tablespoons mild ground chile
1 tablespoon oil
2 pounds lean ground beef
3 cloves garlic, minced or pressed
1/2 onion, chopped
1 (14 1/2 ounce) can of tomato sauce
3 cups water
1 1/2 teaspoons ground cumin
1 1/2 teaspoons oregano
1 1/2 teaspoons salt
1 1/2 teaspoons paprika
1 1/2 teaspoons ground red pepper (optional)

12 corn tortillas
oil for frying
1 pound cheddar or Longhorn style cheese, grated
1 onion, finely chopped

Chili

Wash chiles, remove the stems, slit open and remove the seeds. Simmer in hot water until skin loosens (about 1 hour). Cool. Carefully peel off skins and discard. Puree pulp in a blender or food processor.

Brown the meat in a hot skillet with oil, garlic, and onion. After the meat turns dark, stir in flour, then add the tomato sauce, water and the remaining ingredients. Add the chile pulp or ground chile. Simmer for 1 hour.

Enchiladas

Heat oil in a skillet. Dip each tortilla, one at a time, in the oil to soften. Note, you may also heat the tortillas by placing them in a microwave safe dish, covering tightly with plastic wrap, and cooking in the microwave on the reheat setting for 2 minutes. This reduces the fat content and calories.

Place 1 tablespoon chili, 1 tablespoon grated cheese, and 1 teaspoon chopped onion on one side of the tortilla. Roll up tightly and place seam side down in a 9 x 13 inch greased casserole dish. After all the tortillas have been rolled, pour the remaining chili over the top. Sprinkle with the remaining cheese and onion.

Bake at 350° for 30 minutes until bubbly and the cheese has melted.

Serves 6

FAJITAS

Fajitas are a soft taco that is filled with meat that has been marinated, grilled and thinly sliced. Both beef and chicken fajitas are popular. The meat is wrapped in a warm flour tortilla and topped with a choice of pico de gallo, chopped onion, guacamole, grated cheddar cheese and sour cream. The meat is served sizzling hot on a fajita skillet, and guests can fill their own tortillas. At many local celebrations fajitas are served buffet style as a main dish. The meat and toppings make a great presentation. Fajita fever has been around for a long time in San Antonio and is now catching on all over the country.

CHICKEN FAJITAS

Marinade
1 teaspoon freshly ground black pepper
2 cloves garlic, minced or pressed
3 tablespoons olive oil
3 tablespoons red wine vinegar
1 teaspoon fresh lemon or lime juice
1 teaspoon Worcestershire sauce
1 teaspoon oregano

Meat
1-1 1/2 pounds boneless, skinless chicken breasts
1 tablespoon oil
1 onion, cut in 1/4 inch strips and separated into rings
1 green or red sweet bell pepper, cut into 1/4 inch strips

Toppings
1 cup grated cheddar cheese
1 cup sour cream
1 cup Pico de Gallo (see page 129)
1 mashed avocado, mixed with juice of 1/2 lime (guacamole)
12 flour tortillas

Mix the marinade ingredients and pour over chicken. Let stand in refrigerator 1-2 hours. If you have less time, marinade out of the refrigerator for 15-20 minutes. Discard marinade.

Heat 1 tablespoon oil in a large skillet on medium-high setting. Add marinated chicken breast, sliced onion and pepper. Sauté, stirring constantly, until the meat is cooked and the onion is clear.

Heat tortillas individually on a hot griddle or pan, turning once. They should be soft and not crispy. You may also heat the tortillas by wrapping them in foil and heating in the oven at 350° for 15 minutes or until heated thoroughly.

Fill tortillas with 1 or 2 strips of meat and desired toppings. Roll the tortilla and serve immediately.
Serves 6

BEEF FAJITAS

Marinade
1/2 cup lime juice
2 cloves garlic, minced or pressed
1 teaspoon freshly ground black pepper
1/4 cup olive oil
1 teaspoon Worcestershire sauce

Meat
2 1/2 pounds beef skirt or flank steak
charcoal (preferably mesquite) or mesquite hard wood

Toppings
1 cup grated cheddar cheese
1 cup sour cream
1 cup Pico de Gallo (see page 129)
1 mashed avocado, mixed with juice of 1/2 lime (guacamole)

Combine and mix marinade ingredients in a shallow, non-metallic dish. Add steak and turn over several times to coat. Cover and place in refrigerator to marinade 1 to 2 days. Toss several times to keep meat covered while marinating.

Grill steak over hot fire, 5 minutes on each side, or until it reaches desired doneness.

Meanwhile heat tortillas on a hot griddle or skillet until soft and warm, turning once. (You may also heat in oven, wrapped in foil, at 350° for 15 minutes). Cover tortillas to keep warm.

Remove steaks from fire and cut in strips, 1/2 inch thick, across the grain.

Each person assembles their own taco by filling with 1 or 2 strips of meat and the desired toppings.

Serves 6

KING RANCH CHICKEN CASSEROLE

This recipe comes from the great King Ranch of South Texas. It makes a lovely casserole dish that is easy to prepare on short notice.

1 large fryer, boiled in water seasoned with salt and pepper
1 onion, chopped
1 green sweet bell pepper, chopped
1 clove garlic, minced or pressed
1 can cream of mushroom soup
1 can cream of chicken soup
1 cup reserved chicken broth
1 can tomatoes with green chilies, diced
2 cups grated cheddar and/or Monterey Jack cheese
1 dozen corn or flour tortillas sliced in 1 inch strips

Debone chicken and shred with fingers into bite-sized pieces. Set aside.

Combine soups, chicken broth and Rotel tomatoes to make a sauce.

Sauté onion, pepper and garlic until tender.

In a large, oiled casserole dish layer chicken, sauce, tortillas, sautéed vegetables and cheese. Repeat layers ending with cheese. Bake at 350° for 30 minutes or until bubbly.

Serves 6-8

POLLO EN MOLE

Mole is the most distinctive sauce I have ever tasted. It is very dark in color and rich in taste. You may use bottled mole sauce that can be found in the Mexican food section of your grocery store instead of making your own.

2 whole chickens, cut up (or 4 whole chicken breasts)
2 stalks celery
1 carrot, quartered
1/2 onion, coarsely chopped
2 teaspoons salt

Mole
4 ancho chiles
4 pasilla chiles
2 onions, quartered
2 cloves garlic, peeled
3 tablespoons blanched almonds
1/4 cup raisins
1/4 teaspoon coriander
1/4 teaspoon ground clove
1/4 teaspoon cinnamon
1 teaspoon chopped cilantro
1 tablespoon sugar
1 (14 1/2 ounce) can tomatoes, diced
1 tortilla
1/4 cup olive oil
2 ounces bitter chocolate
1/2 teaspoon salt
1 (14 1/2 ounce) can chicken broth or 2 cups reserved stock
        from poaching the meat

Cover chicken with water in a large pot. Add celery, carrot, onion and salt. Cook until tender. Let cool.

Wash chiles. Remove seeds, stems and veins. Simmer in 2 cups of hot water for 1 hour. Add remaining ingredients, (except oil, chocolate, salt and chicken broth) in a blender and puree until smooth. This may need to be done in several batches because it may overfill the blender.

Heat the oil in a large skillet. Cook the blended mixture in the oil 5 minutes, on medium heat, stirring constantly. Add the reserved 2 cups of broth and the chocolate. Add salt to taste. Cook until the sauce is thickened and the chocolate is melted.

Add pieces of chicken and simmer for 30 minutes, basting frequently.

Serves 6.

Note, although mole is traditionally prepared as a sauce for chicken, it can also be used with turkey and is a great dish for leftover turkey.

MENUDO

Menudo is a Tex-Mex favorite. It is said to relieve the symptoms of a hang over.

2 pounds of tripe
6 cloves of garlic, pressed
1 large can of hominy
1 teaspoon cumin
4 tablespoons chili powder
2 teaspoons oregano
1 pound pork knuckles
salt and pepper to taste

Cut tripe into 3 inch pieces and rinse in warm water. Place in pot and cover with water. Season with salt and pepper. Bring to a boil and simmer for 2 hours or until tripe is tender.

In another pot, cook pork knuckles in enough water to cover, for one hour. Add seasonings and blend well. Add this to tripe. Add hominy and boil for 10 minutes. Serve with tortillas and top with chopped onion and lemon juice.

TACOS

Tacos are another main dish in San Antonio cooking. They are made in a variety of styles: soft, crispy, breakfast, dinner, chicken, beef, and the list goes on. They consist of a tortilla, corn or flour, that is filled with meat and toppings. Use warmed flour tortillas for soft tacos and fried corn tortillas for crispy.

The types of tacos are so extensive I am sure you will find at least one to suit your tastes. Children love to eat tacos and love making them also.

CRISPY BEEF TACOS

1 1/2 pounds lean ground beef
1 teaspoon salt
1 1/2 tablespoons flour
1 1/2 tablespoons chili powder
1 1/2 cups water
1/2 teaspoon ground cumin
1 clove garlic, minced or pressed
oil for frying tortillas
12 corn tortillas

Toppings
1 cup cheddar cheese, grated
1/2 cup chopped onion
1 cup shredded lettuce
1 tomato, chopped
salsa or bottled picante sauce

Brown ground beef in a large skillet, crumbling with a spoon while cooking. Drain.

Add salt, flour, chili powder, water, cumin and garlic. Stir until blended. Simmer over medium heat until thickened, stirring occasionally. Set aside.

Heat 1/2 inch oil in skillet. Hold one tortilla with tongs and dip one side in the oil until browned. Then, dip the other side in the oil and brown, while holding the edges apart to form a pocket. Drain on paper towels.

Fill individual taco shells with meat filling. Top with your choice of toppings.

Serves 6

CRISPY CHICKEN TACOS

2 chicken breasts, poached 20 minutes in water and 1/2
teaspoon salt
2 tablespoons oil
1 medium onion, chopped
1 clove garlic, minced or pressed
1 can chopped tomatoes and green chiles
1/2 teaspoon cumin
1/2 teaspoon salt, if needed
12 corn tortillas
oil for frying tortillas

Toppings
1 cup cheddar cheese, grated
1/2 cup chopped onion
1 cup shredded lettuce
1 tomato, chopped
salsa or bottled picante sauce

Shred chicken breast meat with fingers, or chop coarsely.

Sauté onion, garlic and shredded chicken in oil until onion is
clear and chicken is browned.

Add tomatoes and green chiles, with juice, and seasonings. Cook
over medium heat until liquid is absorbed (about 10 minutes).

Heat 1/2 inch oil in skillet. Hold one tortilla with tongs and dip
one side in the oil until browned. Then dip the other side of the
tortilla in the oil and brown, while holding the edges apart to
form a pocket. Drain on paper towels.

Fill individual taco shells with meat filling and your choice of
toppings. Serve immediately.

Serves 6

SOFT TACOS

The soft taco is to San Antonians as the crepe is to Parisians. It can be made for any meal, including breakfast (see section on Breakfast Dishes). They are served in a tortilla that has been warmed on a hot griddle or pan, turning once. This makes the tortilla soft and easy to fold. You can also warm the tortillas by wrapping them in foil and heating in a 400° oven for 20 minutes.

TOPPINGS

Soft tacos can be served with many different toppings. Just experiment and fill the tortillas with any combination that you like.

shredded cheddar or Monterey Jack cheese
sour cream
chopped onion
guacamole
pico de gallo
salsa
green salsa
chopped cilantro

BEEF BRISKET TACOS

Rub a trimmed beef brisket with a mixture of 2 teaspoons salt, 2 teaspoons coarsely ground black pepper and 2 teaspoons paprika. Cover meat and let marinate in the refrigerator overnight. Cook over mesquite wood or charcoal for 6 hours. Slice across the grain and use with toppings to fill tacos.

CARNE GUISADA TACOS

2 tablespoons oil
2 pounds cubed round steak
1/2 bell pepper, chopped
1/2 onion, chopped
2 cloves garlic, minced or pressed
1 tablespoon flour
1/2 tablespoon ground black pepper
1 teaspoon cumin
1 (8 ounce) can tomato sauce
1 1/2 cups water

In a large skillet, brown meat in oil. Add bell pepper, onion and garlic and sauté until onion is clear. Add flour and brown, stirring constantly. Add black pepper and cumin. Blend in tomato sauce and water. Simmer 10-15 minutes. Use meat to fill tortillas with choice of toppings.

SOFT CHICKEN TACOS

2 chicken breasts, poached 20 minutes in water and 1/2
teaspoon salt
2 tablespoons oil
1 medium onion, chopped
1 clove garlic, minced or pressed
1 can chopped tomatoes and green chiles
1/2 teaspoon cumin
1/2 teaspoon salt, if needed

Shred chicken breast meat with fingers, or chop coarsely. Sauté
onion, garlic and shredded chicken in oil until onion is clear and
chicken is browned. Add tomatoes and green chiles, with juice,
and seasonings. Cook over medium heat until liquid is absorbed
(about 10 minutes). Use meat to fill tortillas with choice of toppings.

FAJITA TACOS
(See recipes above at pages 83 and 84)

REFRIED BEAN AND CHEESE TACOS

Prepare one recipe of refried beans, page 108. Grate enough
cheddar cheese to fill tortillas. Fill heated tortillas with warmed
refried beans and grated cheddar cheese. Fold over and enjoy.

PICADILLO TACOS

1/2 pound ground beef
1/2 pound ground pork
1 small onion, chopped
1 cup water
1 teaspoon salt
1/2 teaspoon cinnamon
1 teaspoon sugar
1/2 teaspoon paprika
1/2 teaspoon oregano
1/2 teaspoon cumin
2 cloves garlic, minced or pressed
1 small can tomato paste
1 large (14 1/2 ounce) can diced tomatoes
3 small, peeled potatoes, diced
1 small jar diced pimentos
1/2 cup raisins
3 jalapeño peppers, seeded and minced
1/2 cup slivered almonds, toasted

Brown meat with onion until onions are clear. Drain. Add water, seasonings, garlic and tomato paste. Mix well and simmer, covered, for 30 minutes. Add remaining ingredients, except almonds. Stir and simmer for another 30 minutes. Add almonds and simmer for another 10 minutes. Serve hot with warmed tortillas.

This recipe is also great as an appetizer served with tortilla chips.

TAMALES

Tamales are a real San Antonio tradition. They are always eaten at Christmas eve celebrations as well as at other fiestas throughout the year. Friends and family work together to assemble the tamales, a "tamalada", making the job a fun activity.

You can use beef, chicken or pork in the following recipe, as desired. The filling may be made a day ahead of time and refrigerated overnight. To simplify the dish, you may use canned red chile sauce instead of fresh, but the taste will not be the same. The spiciness of the sauce is determined by the type of red chile you use. Ancho and pasilla chiles are milder, while cascabel and New Mexico chiles are hotter.

Tamales can be made ahead of time and frozen. After thawing, the tamales should be steamed.

To gage your yield, one pound of meat and one pound of masa should yield 12 tamales. This varies, however, according to how much you put into each tamale.

3 1/2 pounds whole chicken
3 1/2 pounds pork roast (with bone)
2 1/2 pounds corn husks
24 dried red chile pods
4 cups water
2 teaspoons salt
1 large onion, chopped
3 cloves garlic, minced or pressed
7 tablespoons salt
2 tablespoons melted lard or bacon drippings
5 pounds masa harina (ground corn flour)
1 1/2 pounds lard (not shortening)
5 tablespoons baking powder
5 tablespoons salt
3 cups meat broth, reserved from cooking meat filling

Boil chicken and pork roast together and cook until meat falls off the bone. Cool.

Wash corn husks in warm water and leave to soak until ready to use.

Wash red chile pods and remove stems and seeds. Bring water to a boil. Add chiles and simmer 10-20 minutes. Pour all into a blender. Strain to remove skins. Add 2 teaspoons of salt. This should make 4 cups of red chile sauce.

Sauté onion and garlic in 2 tablespoons of lard; add 1 cup of broth and 2 cups of red chile sauce and 2 tablespoons of salt. Simmer for 20 minutes.

Chop the meat fine for the filling. Combine with enough red sauce to moisten into a paste.

Whip 1 1/2 pounds of lard to the consistency of whipped cream. Mix with masa. Add baking powder and 5 tablespoons of salt. Beat until mixture is very fluffy. Add 2 cups of red chile sauce and 2 cups of broth, blending well. You may add more broth if needed to make masa spreadable.

Spread husks with masa and filling by placing 1 tablespoon masa in the middle of the husk and spreading toward the outside edges. The cut end of the corn husk is used as the top and the pointed end is used as the bottom. Spread closer to the top of the husk than the bottom.

Spread 2 tablespoons of the filling in the middle of the masa lengthwise. Roll the husk and overlap the sides. Fold the bottom up 1 1/2 inches and place on a flat surface, folded side down. Repeat for the rest of the tamales.

Place the tamales in a steamer, standing upright. Cover with additional husks or foil. Cover tightly and steam 2-3 hours. They will be done when you can unroll the tamale without it sticking to the husk.

Yields approximately 6 dozen

TAMALE PIE

A truly Tex-Mex concoction, this Tamale Pie recipe makes a festive casserole sure to satisfy the urge for Tex-Mex food.

1 dozen tamales, shucked
3 chicken breasts, poached, boned and shredded
1 onion, chopped
1 clove garlic, minced or pressed
1 green bell pepper, seeded and chopped
1 tablespoon olive oil
1 (15 ounce) can tomato sauce
1 (4 ounce) can black olives, sliced
2 tablespoons ground chile or chile powder
1 (14 1/2 ounce) can cream style corn
8 ounces cheddar cheese, grated

Oil a 9"x13" casserole dish. Line the bottom with tamales. Layer the chicken on top. Sauté onion, garlic and bell pepper in olive oil. Add tomato sauce, olives, chile and corn. Blend well and pour over chicken. Sprinkle cheese on top. Bake at 350° for 1 hour or until bubbly.

Serves 6-8

Side Dishes

SIDE DISHES

BORRACHO BEANS

This recipe uses beer making the beans "drunk" or "borracho".

1/2 pound bacon, fried and crumbled, reserving 2 table-spoons of drippings
1 onion diced
2 cloves garlic, minced or crushed
2 jalapeño peppers, seeded and minced
1 pound pinto beans, soaked overnight and cooked
2 cans of beer
salt and pepper to taste

Sauté onion, garlic and jalapeño in bacon drippings until clear. Add cooked beans and beer. Salt and pepper to taste. Simmer until bubbly. Crumble bacon over top. Serve hot. Add water if necessary to keep mixture liquid.

Serves 6-8

CALABACITA CASSEROLE

Calabacita, or Mexican squash, is a wonderfully flavorful vegetable. If available fresh you should use it in this recipe. Otherwise, you may substitute zucchini squash.

1 1/2 pounds calabacita or zucchini squash, chopped
1 tablespoon onion, minced
1 clove garlic, minced or pressed
1/2 stick of butter, divided
1 (14 1/2 ounce) can diced tomatoes
1 cup grated Monterey Jack or other Mexican style cheese
1 (15 ounce) can whole kernel corn
4 eggs, beaten
salt and pepper to taste
1/2 cup bread crumbs

Steam squash until tender. Sauté onion and garlic in 2 tablespoons butter until onion is clear. Add tomatoes and cook 5 minutes. Add squash, cheese and corn. Cool slightly and add eggs. Season with salt and pepper. Pour into greased casserole dish. Cover with bread crumbs. Slice remaining butter and place on top. Bake at 350° for 30 minutes.

Serves 6-8

CORN CUSTARD

Yum! Everyone will love this corn side dish. Corn, chiles and cheese together make a great combination.

4 eggs beaten
4 cans (8 cups) cream style corn
1 1/2 cups corn meal
1 1/2 teaspoons salt
1 clove garlic, minced or pressed
1 teaspoon baking powder
3/4 cup melted butter
2 (4 ounce) cans diced green chiles
1 tablespoon sugar
1 1/2 cups cheddar cheese, grated

Heat oven to 375°. Combine all ingredients, blending well. Pour into a greased large casserole dish. Bake for 1 hour or until a knife inserted in the center comes out clean.

Serves 10-12

FIDEO

Fideo is a thin pasta that makes a wonderful side dish with Tex-Mex seasonings.

1 package Vermicelli pasta (10 ounces)
1/4 cup cooking oil
1 can whole tomatoes
2 cloves garlic, minced or pressed
3 cups boiling water
1/2 teaspoon cumin
1/2 teaspoon freshly ground black pepper
1/4 cup green bell pepper, chopped
2 teaspoons salt

Fry vermicelli in oil until golden brown. Add, tomatoes, garlic, water, spices, bell pepper, and salt. Simmer 15 to 20 minutes.

Variations. Cooked chicken, ground beef or pork may be added to make this a main dish.

Serves 4-6

GREEN CHILE AND RICE CASSEROLE

Once you make this casserole the first time you will make it again and again. It is great with any entree.

1 1/2 cups long grain rice
1 tablespoon butter
1 jalapeño pepper, finely minced (optional)
1 onion, chopped
1 (8 ounce) can peeled green chiles
1 cup sour cream
1 cup cheddar cheese or Monterey Jack cheese, grated

Cook rice according to directions, and set aside. Sauté onion and jalapeño pepper in 1 tablespoon butter, until onions are clear. Layer in a oiled 9x13 inch casserole as follows: rice, onions, green chiles, sour cream and cheese. Repeat layers if you are using a deep casserole dish.

Bake at 350° for 20-30 minutes or until cheese has melted.

Serves 8-10

JICAMA

Jicama is nicknamed "the Mexican potato". It's skin is brown and the white meat is crisp and juicy, somewhat like a water chestnut. It is frequently served raw and is a light, refreshing accompaniment to Mexican food.

1 medium sized jicama
1/3 cup fresh lime juice
2 tablespoons chili powder
2 tablespoons seasoned salt

Peel and slice jicama. Soak with lime juice. Blend the seasonings and dip jicama in the seasonings. Serve as a side dish or appetizer.

MEXICAN GRITS CASSEROLE

The Tex-Mex flavors in this recipe turn ordinary grits into an exciting, flavorful dish. You can omit the jalapeños if they are too strong.

2 cups quick grits
2 cups grated cheddar cheese
1 stick (1/2 cup) butter
3 eggs well beaten
2 jalapeños, seeded and minced fine
2 dashes Tabasco sauce
1 teaspoon garlic salt
1 (4 ounce) can diced green chilies

Cook grits according to package directions. Remove from heat and add remaining ingredients, blending well.

Pour into oiled 9" x 13" casserole pan. Bake at 350° for 1 hour.

MEXICAN HOMINY

Hominy is a type of corn that is boiled for cooking. In this recipe, it has an exciting Tex-Mex flavor.

1 medium onion, chopped
2 cloves garlic, minced or pressed
1/2 pound of bacon
2 (16 ounce) cans white hominy
1 (14 1/2 ounce) can chopped tomatoes
3 tablespoons chili powder
1 cup grated cheddar cheese

Sauté onion, garlic and bacon until bacon is crisp and onions are clear. Drain off the fat. Crumble bacon. Return to pan.

Add hominy, tomatoes and chili powder. Cook over low heat until creamy. Pour into 9" x 13" casserole and top with grated cheese. Bake at 350° for 30 minutes or until heated through.

Serves 10-12

SPANISH RICE

Spanish rice is a widely used Tex-Mex side dish. This is an authentic version you can use with any Tex-Mex meal.

1/4 cup oil
1/2 onion, chopped
1 clove garlic, minced or pressed
2 ribs of celery, finely chopped
1/2 sweet bell pepper, finely chopped
1 cup uncooked rice
1 can peeled tomatoes, chopped
1/2 teaspoon ground cumin
1 tablespoon chili powder
1 (10 1/2 ounce) can chicken broth

Cook onion, garlic, celery, bell pepper and rice in skillet until vegetables are tender and rice is browned. Add tomatoes, spices and chicken broth. Bring to a boil, reduce heat, and cover with lid. Simmer at low temperature, undisturbed, for 17-20 minutes or until all the liquid is absorbed.

Variation: You may add 1/2 pound chorizo or other pork sausage that is browned and drained.

Serves 4-6

REFRIED BEANS

This is the most widely used and versatile side dish in Tex-Mex cooking. Serve refried beans as a dip with chips, as a taco filling or as a side dish in any Mexican meal.

3 tablespoons bacon drippings
4 cups cooked and drained pinto beans
2 cloves garlic, minced or pressed
salt to taste
1/2 teaspoon cumin (optional)

Heat bacon drippings in a heavy skillet on medium heat. Add the beans and mash them with a potato masher or fork until thoroughly crushed. Add garlic, salt and cumin.

Cook for 20 minutes, or until heated through.

Serve hot.

Serves 6-8

TOMATOES, CHILES AND CHEESE

This recipe makes a light accompaniment to a hearty Tex-Mex meal.

1 (16 ounce) can whole tomatoes
1 cup sour cream
1/2 teaspoon salt
1 tablespoon flour
1/4 cup minced onion
1 (4 ounce) can diced green chiles
1 cup grated cheddar or Monterey Jack cheese

Cut tomatoes in thick slices. Mix remaining ingredients, except cheese, blending well. Place tomatoes in a shallow baking dish that has been prepared with oil. Cover evenly with sour cream mixture. Top with grated cheese. Broil about 4 minutes or until cheese is melted.

Serves 8

BREAKFAST DISHES

BREAKFAST TACOS

Breakfast tacos are a great way to start the day in San Antonio. The variety is as extensive as the number of fillings. To begin, the tacos are made with a flour tortilla that is warmed. The traditional way to warm the tortillas is to heat them individually on a hot griddle or skillet, turning once. Warm them just enough to make them soft, not crisp. You may also warm them by wrapping them together in foil and heating in the oven at a medium heat for 20 minutes or until heated through. The tortillas are filled and served immediately. Common fillings include: scrambled eggs, grated cheese, chopped ham, crumbled bacon, chorizo sausage and potato. Experiment with the fillings. Breakfast tacos are served with picante sauce, salsa or green chile sauce (see chapter on salsas and condiments).

EGG AND CHEESE BREAKFAST TACOS

1 tablespoon butter
6 eggs beaten
2 tablespoons picante sauce
1/4-1/3 cup grated cheddar cheese
6 flour tortillas, warmed

Melt butter in a large skillet. Cook scrambled eggs in melted butter until firm. Add picante sauce and cheese. Stir and cook until cheese is melted. Spoon 2 tablespoons of egg mixture into warmed tortilla. Fold the tortilla and serve immediately.

Serves 6

Variations: Add 2-3 slices of ham to eggs while cooking. Chop and sauté poblano chiles and add to egg mixture. Sauté onion and/or green bell pepper and add to egg mixture.

SAUSAGE AND POTATO BREAKFAST TACOS

1/2 pound chorizo (Mexican sausage) or pork sausage
3 tablespoons oil
1 large potato, diced
1/2-3/4 cup picante sauce
6 eggs beaten
6 flour tortillas

Remove sausage from casing. Brown in skillet, crumbling with a fork. Drain and remove to a paper towel.

Heat oil in skillet. Add potato and picante sauce. Cook until potatoes are tender. Add sausage and eggs and cook until eggs are done.

Warm tortillas individually on a clean skillet and fill with potato mixture.

Add grated cheddar or Monterey Jack cheese if desired.

Serves 6

HUEVOS RANCHEROS

With this recipe you poach the eggs in the sauce. You can, however, scramble the eggs separately and then serve with the tortilla and sauce.

1 onion, chopped
1 clove garlic, minced or pressed
2 teaspoons olive oil
1 (14 1/2 ounce) can tomatoes, diced
salt and pepper to taste
dash of oregano
1/2 of a small can green chiles, diced
4 eggs
4 flour tortillas, warmed
4 ounces Queso Fresco, crumbled (optional)

Sauté onion and garlic in olive oil until onion is clear. Add tomatoes and seasonings and bring to boil. Add eggs and poach in the sauce. To serve, place a tortilla on each plate, put one egg on each tortilla and cover with sauce.

Sprinkle crumbled cheese on top, if desired.

Serves 4

MIGAS

The crumbled or cut tortillas used in this recipe are the "crumbs" referred to in the title. Traditionally, the recipe is made with stale tortillas, that are fried.

4 corn tortillas, crumbled or cut into strips
6 eggs beaten
4 slices of bacon
1/4 cup chopped purple onion
2 tomatoes, chopped
1 jalapeño pepper, seeded and minced
1/2 cup cheddar cheese, grated

Sauté bacon in pan until crisp. Remove bacon and drain on paper towels. Fry tortillas in bacon drippings until crisp. Add remaining ingredients and cook until eggs are set. Crumble bacon and add to the eggs. Serve with warmed flour tortillas and refried beans.

Serves 4-6

TORTILLAS AND BREADS

BOLILLOS

These are a yeast bread roll with a hard crust.

1 package dry yeast
1 3/4 cups luke warm water
1 teaspoon salt
1 tablespoon sugar
6 cups sifted all-purpose flour
oil

Dissolve yeast in warm water. Add salt and sugar. Add flour gradually, 2 cups at a time, stirring well with each addition.

Turn out on lightly floured board. and knead for five to ten minutes. Place in large greased bowl and cover with a cloth. Place bowl in a warm place free from drafts. (An 80-90 degree oven is perfect).

Let dough rise for about an hour or until double in bulk (45 minutes to 1 hour).

Form into about 3 dozen long rolls, twisting each end. Lay rolls on baking sheet. Slit the top of each roll with a knife. Let rise again until double in bulk.

Brush oil on rolls before baking.

Bake in 400 degree oven for 30 to 40 minutes, or until golden brown.

CORN TORTILLAS

4 cups masa harina (corn flour)
1 teaspoon salt
2 1/2 cups warm water (hot tap water is good)

Mix all ingredients to form a dough. The dough should be firm, not sticky or crumbly. Cover dough and let rest for 20 minutes to one hour.

Form dough into about 20, 2 inch balls.

Press each ball to flatten slightly. Place each ball between two pieces of wax paper and roll, using a rolling pin. You may also use a tortilla press. Peel off the top piece of paper and invert. Place the dough into a medium hot skillet that has been lightly oiled, and peel off the remaining piece of wax paper. Cook until browned, turning once. Stack and cover with a soft cloth.

Note: In San Antonio ground red chiles are sometimes added to the corn tortilla batter to make red corn tortillas. They are very festive.

FLOUR TORTILLAS

Flour tortillas are essential to many Tex-Mex dishes such as soft tacos and fajitas. Make sure that they are fresh when you use them. Fresh, store bought tortillas are very good, but if they are not available, this recipe will help you out. Make sure that you roll the tortillas as thin as possible, 1/8 inch thick.

4 cups white flour
1 1/2 teaspoons salt
2 teaspoons baking powder
4 tablespoons vegetable shortening or butter
1 1/2 cups warm water

Combine dry ingredients. Using a fork or fingers, cut in the shortening or butter until well blended and mixture resembles coarse corn meal.

While working the dough with your hands, add half of the warm water. Knead 15 to 20 times. Add the remaining water and knead again. Allow dough to stand 10 minutes.

Form balls with the dough about the size of an egg. Dust each ball with flour and press to flatten. Roll each ball with a rolling pin until it is 1/8 inch thickness and approximately 6 inches in diameter.

Heat a griddle or cast iron skillet on medium heat. Cook tortillas one at a time, turning once. They should be lightly browned, and soft.

Stack the tortillas and wrap in foil. Serve warm.

Makes about 8 to 12 tortillas.

MEXICAN CORNBREAD

Preheat oven 400 °

1 cup white flour
1 cup yellow cornmeal
2 teaspoons baking powder
1/2 teaspoon baking soda
1/2 teaspoon salt
1 teaspoon sugar
3 eggs, beaten
1 1/2 cup milk
3 jalapeño peppers, seeded and chopped
1/2 onion, chopped
1/2 red sweet bell pepper, chopped
1 1/2 cup shredded cheddar cheese
1 teaspoon garlic powder
1 can whole kernel corn, drained
1/4 cup bacon drippings

Combine cornmeal, baking powder, baking soda, salt and sugar. Add egg, milk, peppers, onion, cheese, garlic powder and corn. Heat a 10 inch iron skillet in oven with bacon drippings until melted. Pour batter into hot skillet and bake at 400° for 40 minutes or until golden brown. Serves 10 to 12.

PAN DE CAMPO

This recipe originated on the ranches of South Texas. Pan de Campo is a bread that is made on a fire in a Dutch oven for the cowboys out on the range.

4 cups white flour
5 teaspoons baking powder
3/4 cup shortening
2 teaspoons salt
1 1/2 cups milk

Mix flour, baking powder and salt. Blend in shortening with a fork. Add milk and mix well. Let rest for 10 minutes. Divide dough in half and roll each out to a 10" circle. Place in a greased Dutch oven and bake at 400° until browned. (The traditional way to bake this bread is on hot coals in a Dutch oven.)

Makes 2, 10" loaves

PAN DULCE

Pan Dulce is a sweet bread roll that is topped with a flavored icing.

Dough
1 package yeast
1 teaspoon sugar
1/3 cup of luke warm water
4 cups all purpose flour
1/2 cup sugar
2 tablespoons butter or shortening
1 teaspoon salt
5 eggs, beaten

Topping
1 stick of butter
1 cup flour
1 cup powdered sugar
1 teaspoon vanilla
1 tablespoon cocoa
1/4 teaspoon cinnamon

Dissolve yeast and sugar in warm water. Combine 3 cups of flour, sugar, butter, salt and eggs in a large mixing bowl and mix well. Add remaining flour and mix thoroughly. The dough should be elastic and slightly sticky. Let dough rise in a greased, covered bowl for 1- 1 1/2 hours or until double in size. Punch dough down and shape into 16-24 balls, depending on the size. Place on a greased cookie sheet, 2 inches apart.

For the topping, Blend all the ingredients in a food processor or blender. Remove and shape into a ball. Refrigerate the topping while the dough is rising.

Shape topping into 2 inch balls. Flatten with hands into a circle. Place topping circle on top of each ball of dough, covering the dough. Mark an X on top of each with a sharp knife. Let rise until double in bulk, about 1-1 1/2 hours.

Bake at 350° for 12-15 minutes or until lightly browned.
Makes 16-24 rolls.

SALSAS

Tex-Mex salsas are the essential source of flavor in many dishes. They are either made fresh or cooked. Your tastes will dictate the type of salsa you prefer, some are extremely hot while others are mild. Salsas are usually served in a small bowl on the side of a dish so that each person can add it as they like.

MEXICAN HOT SAUCE (COOKED)

4 serrano peppers, seeded and minced
1 clove garlic, minced or pressed
1 tablespoon oil
1 (14 1/2 ounce) can chopped tomatoes
1 teaspoon sugar
1/2 teaspoon salt
1/4 cup chopped onion (optional)
1 tablespoon chopped cilantro (optional)

Sauté peppers and garlic in oil. Add tomatoes, sugar and salt. Simmer 10 minutes. Add chopped onion and cilantro, if desired.

PICO DE GALLO
"BEAK OF THE ROOSTER"

This salsa, also called Salsa Fresco and Salsa Cruda, is used as a dip served with tortilla chips, and as a condiment with main dishes such as tacos and fajitas.

5 or 6 ripe tomatoes, finely chopped
1 medium onion, finely chopped
2 cloves garlic, minced or pressed
1/4 cup chopped cilantro
Juice of 1/2 lime
1 or 2 (depending on desired heat) serrano peppers, seeded and minced fine
Salt and ground pepper to taste

Combine all ingredients in a bowl and refrigerate or serve at room temperature. Best when served fresh.

SALSA VERDE

1 tablespoon olive oil or bacon drippings
1/2 onion, finely chopped
2 tablespoons flour
1 can chicken broth
1 cup canned green chiles, chopped
1 clove garlic, minced or pressed
1/2 teaspoon salt
1/4 teaspoon ground cumin

Sauté onion in oil or bacon drippings. Add flour and mix well. Add chicken broth, chiles, garlic and seasonings. Simmer 20 minutes.

Serve as an enchilada sauce or as a condiment.

TOMATILLO SALSA VERDE

This salsa is excellent with pork and chicken. The tomatillo is a small green tomato found in the produce section of
your store. They come with a light brown husk which is removed
before using.

1 large onion, chopped
3 cloves of garlic, minced or pressed
3 tablespoons olive oil
1 pound tomatillos (green tomatoes), husks removed and
chopped
1/4 cup chopped fresh cilantro
1 jalapeño seeded and chopped fine, or 1 (4 ounce) can
chopped green chiles
1 teaspoon sugar
1 teaspoon oregano
1 teaspoon basil
1 teaspoon ground cumin
1 teaspoon salt

Sauté chopped onion and garlic in olive oil. Puree tomatillos in
food processor or blender, and add to onion and garlic. Simmer
until soft and thickened. Add cilantro, jalapeño (or chiles), sugar
and seasonings. Continue cooking 10 minutes.

PICANTE SAUCE

Picante sauce is the most well known tomato salsa. It can be found bottled in your store, but making it fresh is even better. This salsa can be used with just about any Tex-Mex dish. With a bowl full of tortilla chips it makes the easiest and best Tex-Mex appetizer.

2 cloves of garlic, minced or pressed
1/2 medium onion, chopped
4 medium tomatoes, peeled and diced
1/4 green or red bell pepper, seeded and diced
1 teaspoon lime juice
1 jalapeño pepper, seeded and minced
salt to taste

Puree all ingredients in a food processor or blender, trying to chop the ingredients without turning them into a liquid. Chop the ingredients by hand if you want a chunky style sauce.

Place in serving bowl and serve with tacos, tostadas, eggs, tortilla chips or most any other Mexican dish. The uses for this salsa are limitless. Keeps in the refrigerator one week.

Salsas

BEVERAGES

FROZEN MARGARITAS

These frozen concoctions are sure to set any social occasion in motion.

1 (6 ounce) can frozen limeade, undiluted
3 ounces Triple Sec
6 ounces Tequila
2 cups of ice
sliced lime quarters
salt

Combine limeade, Triple Sec, Tequila and ice in a blender. Blend on puree until smooth.

Rub the rim of each glass with lime piece. Pour salt into a saucer. Dip the rim of each glass into the saucer of salt, turning to coat evenly.

Pour blended drink into the glasses and serve immediately.

Serves 6

MARGARITAS

This is the official, authentic, Tex-Mex margarita recipe. It's the real thing, but be careful, it is strong.

1 ounce lime juice
1 ounce Tequila
1 ounce Triple Sec liquor
ice
salt
lime slices

Mix lime juice, Tequila and Triple Sec. Pour salt into saucer, covering the bottom. Rub lime slice around rim of glass to wet it. Turn glass over, dip rim in the salt and turn to coat evenly. Fill glass with ice and fill with tequila mixture.

MEXICAN COFFEE

A little Kalhúa and cinnamon turn regular coffee into a fiesta in a cup.

1 1/2 ounce Kalhua or other coffee flavored liqueur
1 cup fresh brewed hot coffee
1 tablespoon whipped cream
A dash of cinnamon

Combine coffee liqueur and hot coffee. Top with whipped cream and cinnamon.

MEXICAN HOT CHOCOLATE

This whipped hot chocolate is a special Tex-Mex treat. Use a molinillo to whip the chocolate if you can find one. It really whips a lot of air into the chocolate.

1/2 cup sugar
3 (1 ounce) squares, unsweetened chocolate or 1/4 cup cocoa powder
1 teaspoon ground cinnamon
1/4 teaspoon salt
2 eggs beaten
6 cups milk
1 tablespoon vanilla extract

In a saucepan, combine all ingredients, except eggs and vanilla. Cook on medium heat until chocolate is melted, stirring constantly. Add one cup of milk mixture to the beaten eggs. Blend thoroughly, then return the egg mixture to the remaining milk mixture. Using a "molinillo" (a Mexican chocolate stirrer), or a fork, whip the chocolate until well blended. You should roll the molinillo between your palms to whip air into the chocolate. Pour into mugs. Garnish with cinnamon sticks, a spoonful of whipped cream, and/or a dash of nutmeg. Serve immediately.

Serves12

SAN ANTONIO BLOODY MARIA

1 1/2 cups tomato juice
1/4 cup chopped onion
1 clove garlic
1 teaspoon Worcestershire sauce
1/2 teaspoon salt
1/2 to 1 teaspoon jalapeño juice
3 ounces tequila

Combine tomato juice, onion, garlic, Worcestershire sauce, salt and jalapeño juice in blender and puree until smooth. Strain and pour into ice filled glasses. Add 1 ounce of tequila to each glass and stir.

Warning. Be careful with the jalapeño juice, it can be very hot.

Serves 2

SANGRIA

Ol' Jerry Jeff made much ado about Sangria wine. The fruit floating in the mixture makes a festive presentation when served in a large clear pitcher.

4 oranges
2 lemons
2 limes
1 cup sugar
1 liter of dry red wine
15-20 ounces of club soda

Cut oranges, lemons and limes into thin slices. Squeeze juice from the slices into a pitcher. Add slices and sugar to the pitcher. Stir well. Add wine and club soda. Stir and pour into tall, ice-filled glasses. Garnish with orange slices.

Makes 4 quarts

TEQUILA SUNRISE

The red and orange colors in this mixed drink look like a beautiful Texas sunrise.

3/4 cup of orange juice
2 ounces tequila
crushed ice
1 ounce grenadine

Fill glasses with ice. Combine orange juice and tequila, blending well. Pour into glasses. Slowly add grenadine, letting it go to the bottom.

Beverages

The Tex-Mex Cookbook

DESSERTS

ARROZ CON LECHE
(RICE PUDDING)

1/2 cup rice
1 cup water
pinch of salt
4 cups milk
1 cup sugar
1/2 teaspoon cinnamon
1 tablespoon butter
1/2 cup raisins
1/2 cup slivered almonds, toasted

Bring rice, water and salt to a boil. Cover and reduce heat to a simmer. Cook covered 15 to 17 minutes, until the water is absorbed. Add milk, sugar, cinnamon, and butter and cook until all the milk has been absorbed. Add raisins and almonds, reserving some for garnish. Turn onto a serving dish and sprinkle with reserved raisins and almonds. Chill. Serve cold.

Serves 6

BUÑUELOS

Buñuelos are a traditional, festive Mexican dessert. The Mexican custom is to serve buñuelos on cracked pieces of pottery during the holiday season, and for good luck a dish should be broken for every buñuelo eaten.

12 flour tortillas
oil for frying
1/2 cup sugar
1 teaspoon cinnamon

Heat enough oil in skillet to measure 3 inches deep. Fry tortillas in oil until crisp, one at a time, turning once. Drain on paper towels. Mix sugar and cinnamon. Sprinkle tortillas with cinnamon sugar. Serve with ice cream or fruit.

Makes one dozen buñuelos.

MEXICAN CHOCOLATE CAKE

1 stick of butter
1/2 cup oil
2 ounces (2 squares) of unsweetened chocolate
1 cup water
2 cups flour
1 teaspoon baking powder
2 cups sugar
1/2 cup buttermilk
2 eggs, beaten
1 teaspoon cinnamon
1 teaspoon vanilla

Preheat oven to 350°. In a small saucepan, combine butter, oil, chocolate and water and heat until chocolate is melted. Combine remaining ingredients in a mixing bowl. Blend in the chocolate mixture. Pour into a greased 9" x 13" pan. Bake for 20-25 minutes. Ice with Mexican Chocolate Icing, recipe follows.

MEXICAN CHOCOLATE ICING

1 stick butter, softened
2 squares (2 ounces) unsweetened chocolate
1/4 cup milk
1 pound powdered sugar
1 teaspoon vanilla
1/2 cup chopped pecans

Combine butter, chocolate and milk in a small saucepan. Heat until butter and chocolate melt. Remove from heat and gradually add powdered sugar, vanilla and pecans. Blend thoroughly and ice cake while still warm.

FLAN

Flan is a classic Mexican custard dessert. Its smooth, light texture makes it the perfect ending to a Tex-Mex dinner.

1 cup sugar
5 eggs, beaten
1 3/4 cups evaporated milk
3/4 cup sugar
1 cup heavy cream
2 teaspoons vanilla

In a small pan melt 1 cup of sugar and heat until it turns golden brown, stirring constantly. Pour into oven proof pan.

Combine eggs, evaporated milk, sugar, cream and vanilla. Pour into pan with caramelized sugar and place in a larger pan of warm water. Bake at 350° for 1 1/2 hours or until it is firm and a knife inserted in the center comes out clean.

Cool for 10-15 minutes. Invert onto a large serving dish.

Chill in the refrigerator for several hours before serving.

Serves 8-10

MEXICAN WEDDING CAKES

Wedding Cakes are a shortbread cookie coated with powdered sugar, similar to a sand tart.

2 cups flour, sifted
1/2 cup powdered sugar
1 cup pecans, finely chopped
1 teaspoon vanilla
1 stick of butter, softened
1 tablespoon ice water
1 cup powdered sugar for coating

Mix together flour, sugar and nuts. Add vanilla. Cut in butter. If too crumbly, add water, so that dough sticks together. Shape into 1 1/2 inch balls. Place on an ungreased cookie sheet and bake at 350° for 12 minutes. Cool on a wire rack and dredge in powdered sugar until well coated.

Makes 3 dozen cookies

PRALINES

1 cup brown sugar
2 cups white cane sugar
2 tablespoons white corn syrup
1 cup milk
1 stick of butter
4 cups pecan halves or pieces
1 teaspoon vanilla

Heat sugars, corn syrup, and milk to soft ball stage (240 degrees). Add butter, vanilla and pecans. Cool and beat until candy begins to thicken. Drop by tablespoon full on waxed paper. Remove and store in cool dry place.

PUMPKIN EMPANADAS

Empanadas are a Mexican style turnover pastry. Pumpkin is the traditional filling, but you can try other fillings such as sweet potatoes or pie fillings, if you like.

4, 9 inch, pie crusts
1 (16 ounce) can pumpkin or mashed sweet potatoes
3/4 cup sugar
1 teaspoon allspice or pumpkin pie spice
1 egg white
3 tablespoons sugar
1 tablespoon cinnamon

Cut pie crusts into 2 1/2 inch circles with a biscuit cutter. Combine pumpkin, sugar and allspice. Spoon 1 teaspoon of pumpkin mixture in the center of each circle. Fold in half and seal by pinching the edges with your fingers. Brush with egg white and bake on a greased cookie sheet at 450° for 10-12 minutes or until golden brown.

Mix sugar and cinnamon and sprinkle on empanadas. Serve warm.

Makes 4 dozen

SOPAPILLAS

1 cup flour
1/2 teaspoon salt
1 teaspoon baking powder
1 tablespoon sugar
1/2 tablespoon shortening
5 tablespoons milk
oil for frying
honey for coating
1/4 cup sugar and 1/2 teaspoon cinnamon mixed together
for coating

Sift flour with salt, baking powder and sugar. Cut in shortening.
Add milk to make a firm dough. Let stand for 1 hour.

Roll dough 1/4 inch thick on a lightly floured board. Cut with a
small biscuit cutter into circles.

Heat 1 inch of oil in skillet. Fry dough in oil until golden brown,
turning once. Drain on paper towels. Drizzle with honey or
sprinkle with sugar and cinnamon mixture. Serve immediately.

Desserts

The Tex-Mex Cookbook

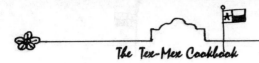